BRADLEY

Wo
From Jo

Frances Hogan is a Catholic scripture teacher who is working as a lay missionary in the Church. She has taught Science and Scripture in West Africa and Ireland for nine years. Since 1975 she has worked full-time as a lay missionary, giving scripture courses, retreats, and working in parishes opening up the scriptures to the people.

Frances Hogan has committed her life to making the Word of God known to lay people in the Church in order to deepen their prayer life and commitment to Christ. She has made a series of Scripture Tapes on books of the Bible and on various spiritual themes.

Available from Fount Paperbacks
by the same author

Words of Life from Exodus

Psalms of Praise: Words of Life from the Songs of Israel

Frances Hogan

Words of Life

From John the Beloved

Collins
FOUNT PAPERBACKS

First published in Great Britain by
Fount Paperbacks, London in 1988

Made and printed in Great Britain by
William Collins Sons & Co. Ltd, Glasgow

Acknowledgements

The author acknowledges the help received from the following books:

The Gospel According to John Volumes 1 and 2: *The Anchor Bible*, by Raymond E. Brown.

The Message of John by the Rev. Thomas E. Crane, Alba House, N.Y.

John, the Different Gospel by the Rev. M. J. Taylor SJ, Alba House, N.Y.

John by the Rev. J. McPolin, SJ, New Testament Message, Veritas.

The Genius of John by the Rev. P. F. Ellis, Liturgical Press.

A Companion to John edited by the Rev. M. J. Taylor SJ, Alba House, N.Y.

Water into Wine by Stephen Verney, Fount Paperbacks.

For Anne Dempsey,
beloved disciple of Jesus,
and my own beloved sister.
In gratitude for a lifetime of friendship,
and for the privilege of sharing
your life's journey.

Contents

Introduction

Everyone agrees that St John's Gospel is a most fascinating document, one which both scholars and saints have commented on, yet one which is the daily bread of all who seek to know Jesus personally in prayer. Among this latter group I have found it is the favourite gospel, even though many find it difficult to understand. It is for this group of ordinary people who are not scholars, that I am writing this book. It is just one way of approaching this marvellous piece of revelation. My hope is that of John himself, that the reading of this book will help you to know Jesus better, and bring you to appreciate our call as "beloved disciples" so that, together, in unity, we may work for the building up of the Body of Christ, and evangelize the world for Him.

To this end I will try to avoid technical references, and keep the book as simple as possible, for it is my firm conviction that the Holy Spirit, who is the main Author of the gospel, carries out the function given Him towards us by Jesus: that of explaining the inner meaning and depth of Jesus' Word. If I pray in the writing of this text, and you pray in the reading of it; then we shall go on a journey of discovery together that will enhance our spiritual lives, and enable us to work more closely as the Body of Christ in the world.

It will be necessary to have a copy of the gospel to hand as you read this book, otherwise you may be a little confused, because I comment on the text in such a way that you will understand some of my comments only if you are looking at the actual text. It would require a much greater volume than this present book if we were to include all the text of John in it.

The text that we call "John's Gospel" in our Bibles is a proclamation of the good news about Jesus and the new Age which he inaugurated, as preached and preserved by one of the Christian groups in the latter half of the first century. It is generally accepted that the gospel had a long and complicated history of development, and that the originator was none other than John, the youngest of the twelve Apostles. The first explicit testimony to this was given by Irenaeus in approximately A.D. 180: "Last of all John, too, the disciple of the Lord who leant against His breast, himself brought out a gospel while he was at Ephesus."

Even a first reading shows that this gospel is very different from the Synoptics. The author gives some material not found in the other gospels, while omitting a lot of material that is contained in them. His interest lies in the meaning of events, not just in recounting them. He is dealing with a young Church in crisis, trying to live its testimony in the Graeco-Roman world, and at the same time seeking to find its identity as distinct from the Jewish traditions in which many of its members grew up. This gospel is written for believers, to root them more deeply into their Christian identity – hence its appeal for those who want to grow spiritually. John wants to help them focus their lives more sharply on Christ, so even when he uses events recounted in the Synoptics, his interest lies in drawing out the inner meaning of the event rather than using it as a mission statement directed at unbelievers.

It is essential for us to penetrate the mystery of who Jesus is as portrayed in the first half of the gospel if we are to grasp who we are called to be as beloved disciples in the second half. It is this double mystery of who He is and who we are that I want to share with you as we journey together through the gospel.

There are two peak points in John that this book seeks to illustrate:
(1) John 1:18 *No one has ever seen God*; *it is the only Son who is close to the Father's heart, who has made Him known.*
(2) John 13:23–25 *The disciple Jesus loved was reclining next to Jesus*; *Simon Peter signed to him and said*, "*Ask who it is He means*", *so leaning back close to Jesus' chest he said*, "*Who is it, Lord?*"

In the first half of the gospel we will learn about the Beloved Son and in the second half about the beloved disciples, a term that I will keep in the plural because it seems that this unnamed disciple represents, not just John as a person, but anyone who wants to enter into the mystery of the body of Christ. It speaks about a particular type of relationship in this gospel.

The gospel begins by showing us the relationship of the Beloved Son to the Father, the one who is close to the Father's heart, therefore always in His presence in a relationship of loving intimacy. John tells us that this Word-become-flesh had this relationship, not just in heaven before time, but also on earth during the days of His incarnation. He was never alone. The Father was always with Him (8:16, 16:32). Not even the greatest of the Old Testament saints had this privilege. Moses did not see God. Even when he was given a partial revelation he was told clearly, "but My face you cannot see, for no human being can see Me and survive" (Exodus 33:18). The Beloved Son has not only seen Him but has been for ever at His side.

The only Son is therefore the only one who can reveal who the Father is, who can speak authoritatively in His Name, reveal His Divine Will, teach His Word and do His works. All this is in the first half of the gospel. In the end the Beloved Son will declare: "*Anyone who has seen me has seen the Father . . . I am in the Father and the Father is in me . . .*" therefore I speak His Word . . . I do His works . . . I reveal His heart . . . in fact "*My Father still goes on working, and I am at work too*" (John 5:18).

The beloved disciples are those who have been with Jesus from the beginning, that is from the time of John the Baptist onwards (chapter 1), those who stay with Him, and gradually enter into an intimate relationship with Him and stay close to Him in prayer (chapters 13 to 16). They are brought into the privileged relationship of a beloved son by adoption through baptism and believing in Jesus (chapters 1 and 3). They are taught how to live as beloved sons in a Community of Love and service (John 13 and 15). They are given the same privileges as Jesus *the* Beloved Son, both in effective prayer and powerful apostolate (John 14). They are sent on Mission to all the world with the power and authority of the Beloved Son (John 20), and the world will receive them just exactly as it received Jesus (John 16). Just as the Father accomplished all that He desired through His only Son (John 19, so too Jesus accomplishes all that He desires through these beloved disciples, who are now endowed with His Spirit (John 20) to teach and guide them into all truth and through all the difficult decisions that lie before them. Jesus passed on everything to His disciples, including His Mission and the privilege of suffering before entering into glory (John 16 and 21).

The challenge to the beloved disciples is to stand before the unbelieving world and declare: "To see us is to see Jesus" . . . we are in Him and He is in us (John 14 and 17) . . . therefore we speak His Word . . . we do His works . . . we reveal His heart to you . . . in fact, as He goes on working so do we! As we set out to investigate this powerful double mystery let us just state for the sake of clarity some of the realities concerning the Beloved Son which will be transposed into His Beloved Community as He sends them into the world *as His presence* to teach, heal, guide, forgive and shepherd His people.

THE BOOK OF SIGNS

The first half of John concerns the revelation of the beloved Son.

THE BELOVED SON IS

The Temple of God . . . (chapter 1); the giver of the Holy Spirit . . . (chapter 2); the Divine Teacher . . . (chapter 3); the Bridegroom of Israel . . . (chapter 3); the Source of Divine Life . . . (chapter 4); the Messiah, and Saviour of the world . . . (chapter 4); the Divine Physician . . . (chapter 5); the Merciful Loving–Kindness of God . . . (chapter 5); our Spiritual nourishment . . . (chapter 6); the Food of the world . . . (chapter 6); the Source of Living Water . . . (chapter 7); the Defender of the weak . . . (chapter 8); the Light of the world . . . (chapter 9); the New Moses, Shepherd of the Flock . . . (chapter 10); the Conqueror of death . . . (chapter 11); the Suffering Servant . . . (chapter 12).

THE BOOK OF GLORY

As Jesus approaches His Hour when He will glorify the Father in His passion and death, the beloved disciples are revealed to us, and we find them an exact replica of the Beloved Son, both as to privilege and mission. They will be His presence on earth, the new People of God with the Holy Spirit dwelling in them, which makes them the Temple of God. They are filled with His Holy Spirit and can impart Him to others, thus passing on the privilege of sonship to future generations. They are sent out to teach the world, to heal, and generally to be the dispensers of the divine grace, or Living Water, made available through Jesus. They provide spiritual nourishment for the world, because they have been charged with feeding the world both spiritually and temporally. They are the defenders and helpers of the weak and helpless, the light of the world. They are also the loving shepherds of Jesus' Flock, who lay down their lives for others both in the daily self-giving of service and in martyrdom whenever it is called for. In general, the mysteries of the life, passion, death and resurrection of Jesus continue in the life, mission, sufferings and glory of His beloved Community of believers, who are totally committed to His Word and work.

This is the mystery we hope to investigate in the study of John's gospel which follows.

Part One

The Book of Signs Reveals the Beloved Son

Chapter 1

The Incarnate Word

The gospel of John is unique from several aspects, not the least being that it begins in heaven, where we are introduced to Jesus as the Word of God. By contrast Mark begins with the public ministry, while Matthew, and particularly Luke, start with the homely events of the infancy narratives. From the very beginning John presents Jesus as divine revelation incarnate. Jesus is shown to be the full expression of God, as the Letter to the Hebrews expresses it: *He is the reflection of God's glory and bears the impress of God's own being* . . . It is this person who becomes flesh in order to share God's own life with us (3:16, 10:10).

Jesus as Wisdom Incarnate

To enable him to express what he wants to say about Jesus, John describes Him in language that the Old Testament used to describe Personified Wisdom. Throughout the gospel he presents Jesus as Wisdom Incarnate. The term John chooses for Jesus is the "Logos", meaning "Word". It indicates that God is revealing Himself in an altogether new and unique way. God had partially revealed Himself through Moses and the prophets, but Jesus is the ultimate revelation, because in Him God is fully revealed (14:9). God's final word to the cosmos, the unbelieving world, is "Jesus".

Just as Wisdom is identified as the Word of God which descended from heaven to execute God's will on earth

(Wisdom 18:14–15), so Jesus is the *Word of God* (Revelation 19:11–16). The Word was understood to carry divine energy, making it effective in its transforming function. We will see this demonstrated in the power of Jesus' word of command in the Book of Signs, where healing takes place even at a distance (4:50, 9:7, 11:43). God's Word was always seen to be life-giving and healing in its effects (Deuteronomy 32:46–47; Psalm 119:37). In Jesus it will be seen to be Spirit-filled and life-giving also (6:63). The Word also enlightens a person interiorly as they begin to live it (Psalm 119:8, 105). Like the rain, God's Word comes down from the realm of "above" to soften our souls, and make them spiritually fruitful before it returns whence it came, having accomplished what it was sent to do (Isaiah 55:11; Psalm 147:15; John 19:30).

John is telling us, then, that what the Old Testament says regarding Wisdom personified is what he is saying regarding the Word Incarnate, in whom, as Paul says, is hidden all the treasures of Wisdom and Knowledge (Colossians 2:2).

Some comparisons between what John says regarding Jesus and what the Old Testament says about Wisdom will throw light on this gospel, for it reveals the backdrop from which John is writing. Wisdom, like Jesus, was with God from the beginning before creation, and, like Him, was involved in creation itself (John 1:1, 17:5; Proverbs 8:22–31; Sirach 24:9). Wisdom is also a pure emanation of the glory of God, as Jesus too manifests the glory of God (John 1:14, 2:12, 17:5; Wisdom 7:25). Wisdom is said to be a reflection of God's everlasting light, but John says that Jesus *is* the light (1:4–5, 8:12, 9:5; Wisdom 7:26; Revelation 21:23). Wisdom descended from heaven and dwelt in Israel as in a Tabernacle (Proverbs 8:31; Wisdom 9:10; Sirach 24:3–8; James 3:15). Jesus, the Word of God, also descended from heaven, from the realm of "above", to "pitch His tent" or tabernacle among us in the incarnation (1:10–12, 14, 3:31, 6:38, 16:28).

Wisdom had a specific mission to teach the people of the things of "above", and to instruct them regarding the will of God in all things. She was the teacher of truth, leading the people to life and immortality, functions that John continuously gives to Jesus throughout his gospel (Job 11:6–7; Wisdom 6:18–19, 23, 9:9, 16–18; Proverbs 4:13). Just as Wisdom taught through long discourses so Jesus will teach in this way, explaining who He is and why He came (Proverbs 8:3–36; Sirach 24). Both will identify themselves with the vine (John 15; Sirach 24:17).

Both Wisdom and Jesus offer their "food", the food of life, in terms of "bread" and "wine", urgently inviting everyone to come and participate in their banquet (6:35, 7:37–39; Proverbs 9:25; Sirach 24:19–21), but there is a difference between Jesus' food which will satisfy all hunger and thirst forever, and that of Wisdom which makes people hunger for more (4:10–14). Jesus will seek out disciples just as Wisdom does, and He will instruct them in the manner of Wisdom, calling them "friends" and "children" since they are given new life by Him (13–17; Wisdom 7:17; Proverbs 8:32–33; Sirach 4:11).

The advent of Wisdom into the cosmos provokes division as many reject her (Proverbs 1:24–25), just as Jesus too will be rejected (1:10–11, 8:46). This rejection means "death" because it thereby closes the people to any further entrance of truth into their lives, and they become blinded, but it is a culpable blindness since it is the result of their own choice (7:34, 8:21, 46, 9:41; Wisdom 6:12; Proverbs 8:17). The coming of Jesus also provokes division and rejection as many prefer the darkness to the light (3:19). Acceptance of both Wisdom and Jesus means "life" to the recipient just as those who reject them court "death". This life and death are not physical, but spiritual, so the consequences are eternal (Proverbs 8:35).

The New Creation

Not only does John speak of Jesus as Wisdom Incarnate, but he situates the gospel against the Creation account in Genesis. Thus the gospel is to be read as the account of the re-creation of human beings, as Jesus strives to restore all that was damaged or destroyed by sin and its effects on the human race. Paradise was lost in the Genesis Creation account, but it will be regained here by Jesus when He is "lifted up" on our behalf, as John will tell us that the Father left everything in the hands of Jesus (13:3). Both accounts begin with the same words: "In the beginning . . . ", but for Genesis it is the beginning of the material creation, whilst for John it is the beginning of the redemption of the world through Jesus the Incarnate Word.

When God created in the beginning He made everything "good" but sin marred the work of His hands. Now after centuries of failure on the part of the Chosen People to live the Word of God and prove its life-giving effects to the unbelieving world, *THE WORD* Himself had come to make a fresh start. Jesus, the Word, was present at the first creation when humans were made in the image of God, their Maker. He had now returned to restore God's image on the earth by giving us a new birth in the Spirit, and calling us to follow Him in a life which will transform us into the image of the Beloved Son (13:17; Romans 8:29). God's first act in creation was to make light to dispel the darkness. Now that light has come in person to deliver us from darkness for ever. Just as the Old Testament reveals that God's many plans and Covenants were in the main rejected by the vast majority of the people, so here it will be no different when the Light of the World is offered.

Thus John, in using the Creation account and the language of Personified Wisdom as his backdrop, finds he can best explain the mysterious divine origins, identity and mission of Jesus, our Redeemer.

Who is this Jesus?

There are three main sections in the first chapter, namely the Prologue, John's witness, and a summary of the discovery of the first disciples of Jesus. We will take the witness of John first and leave the Prologue until last as it is easier to understand that way.

The Witness of John (1:19–34)

The most important question in the gospel is "who *is* this Jesus of Nazareth?" We begin our quest for the answer to this mystery by investigating the first half of John's gospel. We must grasp this before we can even hope to understand the equally fascinating mystery of who the beloved disciples are.

A man came, sent by God. His name was John. He came as a witness, to bear witness to the light, so that everyone might believe through him. He was not the light, he was to bear witness to the light. God sent a great prophet to prepare the way for Jesus, by pointing Him out to the people, and declaring who He was so that they would believe in Him. This shows that God expected everyone to accept Jesus, to follow Him and commit themselves to the way of salvation He offered, as He alone could lead them into the New Age which was dawning.

John the Baptist (JB in future references, to distinguish him from the author of the gospel), came among the people like a new Elijah, having lived most of his life in the wilderness, in prayer and seeking God. He was the prophetic *voice* from the desert that Isaiah had spoken about (Isaiah 40:3–11), who would prepare the way of the

Lord so that the Glory of the Lord could appear among them. The sight of JB excited the people because they recognized the sign of his presence. Thousands responded to the power of his preaching and accepted his baptism. God was really with him.

A delegation of priests and Levites who were specialists in the rites of purification were dispatched from the Sanhedrin to demand an explanation of the new rite of purification introduced by JB. He replied in Isaian terms that he was preparing a way for the Lord, and this called for the levelling of human pride and the filling of their empty lives with God's word so that they would be ready for the Lord's visit. JB was preparing Israel for the greatest divine visitation in her history. God was coming to visit them in the person of the Incarnate Word.

Since this automatically raised expectations regarding the Messiah's coming, it was to be expected that JB would be quizzed about his own identity. They asked: "Who are you?" John declared that he was not the Messiah (the Christ). Their question as to whether he was Elijah referred to the fact that there was a tradition that Elijah would return before the great Day of the Lord (Malachi 3:23–24). If he was not the Christ or Elijah, then maybe he was *the* prophet foretold by Moses (Deuteronomy 18:15–18). John's emphatic "No!" to these questions takes the attention off himself and prepares the people for the One who is to come. The I AM NOT of John prepares us for the I AM of Jesus later, and leaves no confusion, for Jesus is all that JB is not.

JB then explains the difference between himself and Jesus. It is the difference between water and the Spirit, between earth and heaven. JB prepares the people with the water of repentance which was good, for it fulfilled the prophecy of Ezekiel 36:25: *I shall pour clean water over you and you will be cleansed*; Jesus, however, will immerse (baptize) them in the Holy Spirit. Jesus will fill them with the love of God and the Presence of God, having made them children of God (1:12). JB is the voice preparing the people for *the messenger* from God, who will impart God's life to them. Humbly he admits that he is unfit to be the slave of this great personage. All that remains now is for him to point Jesus out to the people.

This he does the following day when he points to Jesus as "the Lamb of God", the one who takes away the sin of the world. In giving this extraordinary title to Jesus, JB reminds us about the suffering servant foretold by Isaiah. Just like that suffering servant, Jesus will be "lifted up". He will also be "familiar with suffering", the one who offers His life in atonement, and who will see His heirs (Isaiah 52–53). The Jewish people, and especially their leaders, could not accept a Messiah who suffers, yet both JB and John's gospel declare that this was God's plan for redemption.

JB also presents Jesus as the Passover Lamb, which was the symbol of redemption (Revelation 5:6; Isaiah 53; Exodus 12; 1 Peter 1:18). Just as the Passover Lamb was chosen four days before being slain, so too the Lamb of God is pointed out some years before Calvary, the new Passover, which celebrates the redemption of the world.

JB admits that he needed a revelation from God to penetrate the mystery of the person of Jesus. Later we will see that everyone who wants to become a disciple will need similar help from God in order to recognize and accept Him. Recognition came for John with the sign of the dove resting on Him. The dove is a symbol of a messenger (Genesis 8:11) pointing Jesus out as God's representative par excellence, the "sent one". Later (3:34) John relates that the Spirit was given to Jesus without measure, so maybe the dove symbolized this also, for JB declared that he saw the Spirit come down *like a dove* and rest on Him. We are reminded also that the Spirit of God hovered over the waters at the Creation of the world, just as He hovers over Jesus now, at the dawn of the New Creation (Genesis 1:1). The resting of the Spirit on Jesus also speaks of the permanence of the gift. The Spirit was *to remain* with Jesus in a unique way. The Spirit would abide in Him, and later He would give the Spirit as a gift to His beloved disciples. The descent of the Spirit on Jesus foreshadows and prepares for the descent of the Spirit on the Church later.

With this declaration we are given a startling new revelation about Jesus. He has come after JB in time, but since He pre-existed him, He therefore outranks him in importance. It was JB's privilege to reveal Jesus to Israel and he now declares Him to be the Chosen One, in whose person the Spirit has come to abide with us on earth, and from this overflowing fountain a floodtide of grace and mercy will flow to the needy in body and spirit.

The First Disciples (1:35–51)

The following day, as Jesus passed by, JB fixed his eyes on Him with penetrating insight, and again pointed Him out to his disciples as the Lamb of God. Two of his disciples responded to this revelation by following Jesus. In this gospel everyone who hears the true message about Jesus is expected to "follow Him", a term used to denote discipleship, (8:12, 10:4, 12:26, 13:36, 21:19, 22). Only in the following, does Jesus reveal Himself, as we see now. He turned around and asked them: *What do you want*? The question was penetrating, for it touched the deepest need in the human person, which is a hunger for God, for the Infinite. If they want to "abide" or "dwell" with the Lord; if they want something that outlasts life, while giving it meaning and direction, then Jesus is interested. "Teacher", they said "where do you live?" Their response is positive. They do want to "abide" with Him, though they must learn that, for Him, this has a deeper significance than they can grasp just now. They do not know that the Prologue reveals to us, the readers, that Jesus now lives among us. He is living in human flesh and it is there, in the Incarnation, that we find Him, but we must penetrate the mystery of His person.

Jesus replied: *Come and see*. They are invited to come to Jesus in faith, and this will enable them to "see" through the mystery of His person so that they can attach themselves to Him as disciples. This is the whole issue of this gospel (3:21, 5:40, 6:35, 37, 40,etc). Their journey of faith begins the moment they begin the "following". Only when they do something about it practically does the mystery unfold: they must go and see, and "stay" or "abide" with Him. From chapter two He will begin to reveal His glory, and as they journey in faith John wants *us* to investigate the signs also, so that when they reach the culmination of their faith in 20:28 we will also say with them *My Lord and my God*!

Their journey of discovery concerning the mystery of Jesus is presented as taking place over a period of days, even though the reality took a long time. John fits it into a pattern of the first week of the New Creation, and this reminder of Genesis helps us to interpret the events that follow. Genesis showed us Paradise lost, John will show how Paradise was regained through Jesus. These disciples do not yet realize that Jesus will enable them to become the inaugurators of a new age.

The first thing Andrew did was to find his brother Peter and testify that they (the other unnamed disciple is usually taken to be John himself) had found the Messiah. They already know that this discovery is not to be kept to themselves. They must act like apostles and bring others to Jesus. The meeting between Simon (Peter) and Jesus is one of the most significant in history. Jesus penetrated Peter's person in one look, and changed his name to "Rock" – Cephas. There is here a hint that Jesus, who is the

Foundation Stone of the Church, would erect the building on this fisherman, for the giving of a new name has a direct relation to the role that person is called to play in salvation history (Genesis 17:5; 32:28). Later, Jesus, the Good Shepherd, will make Peter the shepherd of the flock in his place too (chapter 21).

Jesus called Philip the following day, and he in turn sought out Nathanael, testifying that they had found *Him of whom Moses in the Law and the prophets wrote, Jesus son of Joseph, from Nazareth*. This identifies Jesus as the Prophet-like-Moses of Deuteronomy 18:15–18. The one described by the prophets would be the Messiah, the son of David, or the Son of Man in Daniel, or even the Elijah figure expected by Malachi. Thus they give to Jesus the titles JB had disclaimed for himself. "Son of Joseph" was a normal way of identifying Jesus from any other man of the same name from Nazareth. It does not imply that Jesus *was* the son of Joseph, but only that Joseph was known to be the head of that particular family. Nathanael was not impressed, so Philip extended to him the invitation given to the first disciples – "Come and see". If Nathanael was to become an authentic disciple he would have to experience Jesus for himself, and come to personal knowledge of Him. Only then would he come to know that Jesus is not, in fact, from the backwater town of Nazareth, but from "above", from heaven.

John presents Nathanael as the true Israelite coming to Jesus but finding difficulty in his origins. Jesus helped him to understand by demonstrating His supernatural knowledge of him in his activity under the fig tree. This draws from Nathanael the testimony that Jesus is the Son of God and the King of Israel, the Messianic King (Psalm 2:6–7). Nathanael had believed on a small sign but Jesus promised that he would see greater signs than that, just as He promised Martha later: "If you believe you will see the glory of God" (11:40). The beginning of the "greater things" will be the Book of Signs, but the greatest thing will be His own "lifting up", first on the cross and later in glory in the Book of Glory. Then Nathanael and all others like him will see Jesus as the son of God in the fullest sense, and also king, but King of all nations, not just of Israel.

He then indicated He was the fulfilment of the promise to Jacob/Israel concerning the ladder that would connect heaven and earth (Genesis 28:10–17). He would show them He was that mediator, that in Him all true Israelites would find the goal of their prayer and longing for a redeemer. He referred to Himself as the mysterious Son of Man mentioned in Daniel 7:13. This title is given to Jesus twelve times in the Book of Signs, often as a reminder of His "being lifted up" in order to achieve our redemption.

John does not mention all of the twelve apostles in this section. He is interested only in giving us a summary of what they eventually discovered about Jesus, and in preparing us for the revelation of His glory through His signs – those events through which he would reveal Himself. Since Nathanael is the last to be called, here John indicates that JB's mission "to reveal Jesus to Israel" is now fulfilled. Once Israel comes to Jesus JB can "bow out" gracefully.

The Prologue (1:1–18)

Having received the testimony of the Baptist and that of the first disciples, we can now confidently turn to that of John and his church to complete the picture. Thus we see that this first chapter is, in fact, the revelation of the gospel in condensed form, and will help us interpret what we meet there. Otherwise we would be puzzled by many things through not penetrating beyond the surface to deep hidden truths, for John continuously presents reality on two levels, that of the material level of the cosmos (the unbelieving world) which is mostly blind to the spiritual reality that Jesus presents. In this gospel the cosmos level is called "below", and the spiritual level that Jesus operates on is "above". Power politics, manipulation of individuals and nations, and control of the many by the few, are the principles that operate on the level of "below", while love and self-sacrifice, even to the laying down of one's life, are the principles of "above". It is easy to see why the former is called "death" and the latter "life", and why Jesus is the very symbol of the life from "above".

In the beginning was the Word: the Word was with God and the Word was God . . . through Him all things came into being . . . in Him was life, life that was the light of men . . . and light shines in darkness, and darkness could not overpower it . . . We have heard the Baptist hint at the pre-existence and pre-eminence of Jesus. Now we have the bold statement that He, as the Word, is the full expression of God, eternal and creative. The clear allusion to Genesis – "In the the beginning . . . " – is John's way of declaring the beginning of the new Creation, and also the beginning of the good news about Jesus, the Christ. The clear statement that Jesus is God prepares us for the claim Jesus makes later to be the great "I AM", the One who bears the divine name, when He will use the very same words that God spoke to Moses in Exodus 3:14: EGO EIMI, at the beginning of salvation history.

Everyone has received life from this creative Word. He is the source of life, physical and eternal for all (5:21). All that has been created is intimately bound up with Him, since we came into natural life – and now in the gospel, supernatural life – through Him (Colossians 1:16). Because of this the Word has the right to rule over all creatures (1:10; Revelation 19:11–20; Romans 11:36). This life brings enlightenment too, and cannot be imprisoned in darkness. The great battle between good and evil is fought out in each one of us. If we allow that life of the Word to dominate, then darkness will never overpower it. This holds good for the one as for the many. Later we will see the beloved disciples become this community of light who will be sent out into the darkness of the cosmos where the spiritual warfare will be waged. Already the victory sounds can be heard.

A man came, sent by God. His name was John. He came as a witness, to bear witness to the light . . . he was not the light . . . Normally light does not need a witness, for it can be seen easily. The fact that a witness was required reveals that the light came to blind eyes. It was because Jesus, the Incarnate Word, was coming into the hostile environment of the cosmos that God raised up a testimony to Him in JB, in fulfilment of Isaiah's words (9:1): *The people that walked in darkness have seen a great light . . .* JB's mission could have begun with another passage from Isaiah which was fulfilled in him (60:1–2): *Arise, shine out, for your light has come, and the glory of the Lord has risen upon you. Look! though night still covers the earth and darkness the peoples, on you the Lord is rising and over you His glory can be seen. The nations will come to your light . . .* This prepares us for the next revelation of the prologue.

The Word was the real light, that gives light to everyone; He was coming into the world . . . that had its being through Him and the world did not recognize Him. He came to His own, and His own people did not accept Him. We now witness the advent of the real light into the world (Isaiah 42:6). JB had only been a pointer towards Him. All other lights must now give way before this heaven-sent light. Yet the reality is that He was not received, even by those who were expecting the Messiah. The gospel illustrates this rejection of the Word by His own people (1:11, 4:44, 12:37) and by the cosmos, which was unable to accept Him (1:10, 3:19).

He was not totally rejected, however. *But to those who did accept Him He gave power to become children of God, to those who believed in His name who were born not of human stock or human desire or human will but from God Himself.* Those who did accept Him were constituted children of God by a new birth in the Spirit which had nothing to do with earth. The children of God are born of God. In this way Jesus raises His disciples to live on the level of "above" where love is the overriding principle of action, and creates a new family in the Spirit. This new people of God reflect the life of the Trinity on earth, for it is the descent of *love* that we observe in the coming of the incarnate Word. This love would have to conquer all the egotism that blinds us from comprehending the things of God, and that cripples us spiritually.

The Word became flesh, *He lived among us*, *and we saw His glory*, *the glory that He has from the Father as only Son of the Father*, *full of grace and truth*. The eternal Word entered into human flesh in the person of Jesus, and made His dwelling among us. This is the most awe-inspiring statement that John could make, and in order that its full impact would strike us, He gave a comparison of the "abodes" of the Word. He began by telling us that the divine Word was . . . with God . . . was God (1:1). Now he declares that the Word *BECAME . . . flesh . . . came among us*. No greater contrast is conceivable, for when the Creative Word left His throne of glory He did not just ENTER human flesh, He *became* flesh and took His place in human history (1 John 4:2–3). This humility on the part of the Word is shocking, for when we meet Jesus we meet the divine being who has come to reveal Himself by word and sign. This divine visitation was not in judgement but in mercy, as Jesus came bearing gifts of life, light, bread, love, etc. God has answered our prayers beyond measure. When we could not reach Him, He came down from His glory to live with us as the Father's most precious Son, embodying all of God's Love and Life for us. Grace and truth are God's life and love given to us freely in Jesus. Therefore we shall expect to see those qualities in the ministry of Jesus that the Old Testament declares to be truly God-like, qualities of loving-kindness, mercy and faithfulness to His promises.

When John says that the Word came to live among us he means literally that He made His dwelling or "tent" among us. In Exodus 25:8–9 God asked Moses to make Him a dwelling among His people, and so they constructed the first tabernacle, which was literally a tent. This became the locus of the divine presence among the people of God. Ezekiel 43:7 promised that the Lord would come to live among His people for ever. This found fulfilment when in the incarnation of the Word, the body of Jesus became the locus of God's presence, the new "tent" where the people could meet with God and find life. Thus Jesus is the manifested presence of God, the Shekinah Glory of the Old Testament. To see Him is to see God (20:28) "Glory" (*doxa*) means God's manifested presence. The challenge offered to all who meet Jesus is to penetrate the mystery of His person and "see" this glory.

Indeed from his fullness we have, all of us, received one gift replacing another, for the Law was given through Moses, grace and truth have come through Jesus Christ. Jesus contains within Himself the fullness of God, the fullness of life and love. All that we receive comes from Him as from an overflowing fountain, one gift after another in continuous flow. That Fountain of Life will be opened up on the cross, but already we know the source of the giftedness in the ministry of Jesus, and we will not be surprised to observe people come alive at His touch, or in His presence. Nor will we be taken aback by the power unleashed by His word of command. Moses gave the people religion in the Sinai Covenant, a religion designed to bring them close to God. When Jesus came, God came, bringing the fulfilment that religion hopes for by unleashing God's abundant Life and Love upon all, inaugurating the New Covenant in love. The gift of Moses prepared the way for Jesus and his Law gave way before the forgiving love of the Son.

No one has ever seen God: it is the only Son, who is close to the Father's heart, who has made Him known. Moses had never seen God face to face, for that is not given to humans during their earthly pilgrimage (Exodus 33:18). Jesus is in an altogether different category in that He has seen God for all eternity. Thus the reason why the Son can reveal the Father is because He has been intimately related to Him eternally. Knowing the Father's heart intimately He can speak for Him. He is sent by the Father to carry out His works and reveal His word. The second half of the gospel will reveal the beloved disciple leaning on the heart of Jesus, illustrating that those who are sent on mission by Jesus must know Him intimately also. They, too, having been "with Jesus from the beginning" (Acts 1:21), will be asked to carry out His works and speak His word, continuing His mission on earth, and bearing witness to Him as He did to the Father. Thus the two halves of the gospel have a similar pattern as the relationship of the Son to the Father becomes the pattern of the relationship between Jesus and His beloved disciples.

Chapter 2

The Beloved Son Reveals Himself

We now set out together on a journey with the Beloved Son as He goes to Galilee to begin to unfold the mystery of who He is and why He came. On the way, we, like all the other participants, will be challenged to believe in Him, and to allow Him to change us into disciples. Very quickly we will realize that we must observe events very closely, as things are not what they seem. Very simple happenings have deep and momentous meanings, and John expects us to "read" the setting of the event as part of the revelation, as well as the symbols that he uses to teach us. Even details like the time of day will be significant. We will be initiated into seeing both the "heavenly" and "earthly" aspects of even the simplest things. This is a lesson in discernment which will benefit us in our daily lives where, too, if only we had our eyes opened we would realize that events have a deeper significance than we sometimes acknowledge.

Significantly we begin our spiritual journey "on the third day", and with a wedding. On the human level many will retort "So what!" to both the wedding and the day, as being commonplace. But in a world where God has intervened nothing is ever again commonplace; everything becomes a vehicle of revelation, and a moment of encounter with Him, which has repercussions both for time and eternity. We are on our way to a very momentous happening on the third day after the death of Jesus, the meaning of which can be explained through the wedding symbol.

The Old Testament scriptures describe God the Father as the Bridegroom of Israel, and the Covenant relationship of the People with God as a wedding. They also compare heaven to a wedding banquet (see Isaiah 54:5, 62:5; Jeremiah 3:14; Hosea 2:19). These symbols were used by the prophets to foreshadow the messianic days to come. So when John introduces Jesus at a wedding on the third day he is already hinting at something he will make explicit in chapter three, namely that Jesus is the Bridegroom of the New Israel, and He has come to prepare His Bride for the New Covenant which will be the marriage bond between Himself and the new People of God.

Jesus has come to inaugurate a new age where Love will reign, where men and women will be committed to each other and to God in loving covenant. This is wedding language. Jesus, Incarnate Love, has arrived, bringing in the heavenly dimension. He has brought His disciples who are the new "Bride" in the process of formation. So who is getting married? The village couple make us look at a spiritual reality alive in Jesus and His disciples. The new life being embraced by the young couple indicates the New Age begun in Jesus, where everyone will be called to the marriage of flesh and spirit, of each one and God. And with every new beginning there is past and present reality to tie together. We will see the old order side by side with the new dispensation throughout our journey. The joy and peace of this new relationship with God is signified by the wedding celebrations which in those days went on for a whole week.

Cana (2:1–2)

Jesus and His first disciples had spent the intervening two days on the journey from the Jordan valley to Galilee, arriving in time for the wedding. Jesus was about to reveal Himself to them for the very first time, although neither they nor anyone else had any idea of this. It is understandable that they would find difficulty in seperating the old from the new, but the way to grasp the meaning of the new is to see it through the eyes of the old, since no break exists in the Revelation of God or in Salvation History. As their eyes are opened so too will ours be.

Jesus will transform the old and give it completely new meaning. The old is a worn-out cloak and overstretched wineskins (Mark 2:22). There is no room for change in them. The old wine, which was not the best wine, has run out. It was imperfect just like the old dispensation it stood for. Only the Messiah could give them the overflowing gift of new wine that the prophets had sung about (Amos 9:13; Hosea 2:24; Joel 4:18; Jeremiah 31:12). So we must look for the miracle of transformation here that will point to the need for each disciple to allow the water of their life or the old wine of their past to be transformed by Jesus, so that they can enter upon the new spiritual Way He is opening up for us to walk in the Spirit, and no longer according to the ways of the flesh. As with every marriage, the "cleaving" to the new life only comes with the "leaving" of the old one, but it is more of a transformation than a death, a joy than a sacrifice. In offering us the spiritual marriage God has very definitely kept the best wine until last. That is the reflection of the chief steward, of John, the early Church, and all who have experienced it.

The mother of Jesus was there, and very active too. The title "mother of . . . " someone who was becoming known publicly is a title of honour still used throughout the Middle East. John does not mention Mary by name. He prefers to indicate a deeper reality by using the mysterious title "Woman" which should make us look at her as the second "Eve", the mother of all those who live in the Spirit, and a symbol of the Bride to be (see Genesis 3:15; Revelation 19:7). Here at Cana John indicates that the role of Mary changes with the inauguration of Jesus' ministry. Earthly family ties must be replaced by heavenly ones, the "old family" by the new family.

Mary's role as the human mother of Jesus is over and must give way to the new reality. She is to have no role during His ministry, but her new role will be given during His "Hour" on the cross (19:25–27), where she will be asked to "mother" the disciples into the New Age. He as Head of the New Creation cannot be influenced by merely human considerations, but only by His Father's will. She must become a disciple like the others, receive her instructions from Him, and give the lead in receiving her new role from Him. He expects this transformation in her without explanation, apparently. The disciples must give up family ties and concentrate on their commitment to the "New Family" He is bringing into being. He shows her that He lives what He teaches. Earthly ties must give way before heavenly ones, as the water gives way to the wine at His command.

Noticing that the wine had run out, Mary went to Jesus, even though there is no indication that she had ever before observed a miracle. Her request demanded that Jesus supply the need, but His sharp refusal indicated that things would be different between them now that He had embarked on His official mission. The "Hour" which had not yet come was the time when His full glory would be revealed in His Passion and Death, yet He will give a prophetic sign of it now at her request. Mary, as the New Eve, and the symbol of the Church, the new Bride, would have no role to play until *after* His Hour. Unlike the first Adam, Jesus was not passive before this request, and would remain in full command of His mission.

I wonder whether she hesitated or was just good at "reading" Him? She responded by putting her trust in Him completely, and, as His disciple, gave her first and last command which echoed that of the Pharaoh in Egypt at the time of Joseph. All who came to him for help were sent to Joseph, as he alone had the answer (Genesis 41:55). Mary happily leaves the mission in the capable hands of Jesus without worry or anxiety. He has the answer and He is in control.

This and the signs which follow will show us that Jesus deliberately replaced the old institutions of worship with the new. There were six stone water jars there for the normal ablutions of the Jews. (The number six represents imperfection, since mankind was created on the sixth day and has shown his ability to fail God under every dispensation given to him.) Jesus gave His first command, and all that followed showed that *His word* was different to everyone else's because the effects were dramatic.

He commanded that they should fill the jars with water, the most ordinary and abundant liquid that we have, for God works through the ordinary, bringing about the most extraordinary results from His intervention. He uses everyday things to reach us, and the mundane events of our lives to transform us. Hence we need to keep our eyes open to all that is happening on both the heavenly and earthly levels of reality, in order to know what is going on. We must remember that things are happening at the level of the spirit as well as the flesh. By His action of changing the purification waters at Cana, Jesus, in effect, has "taken over" the purification rites of the Old Testament. His own purification rite will be initiated in His Hour but will be explained before then (13:2–15). Jesus goes from here to purify the Temple also.

The servants are enjoying themselves and they fill the jars to the brim, to overflowing. The one hundred and twenty gallons reflects the abundant new life that Jesus is about to give. The "water" of the Old Testament is not cast aside, but is transformed into the new wine of the Kingdom of God. Were they expecting a miracle or did they think Jesus was playing a joke? He commanded them to take some to the president in charge of the feast, who, when he had tasted the water, exclaimed to the bridegroom, that the normal procedure at such events was to serve the best wine first when tastes were sharp, and the inferior type later when it would not be so obvious. "*But you*", *he said* "*have kept the best wine until now*!" John observes that the man had no idea where this wine had come from, but he expects his readers to know, *and* why it is the best there is.

This will be a recurring theme with us as we journey on. People will not realize where the new life comes from, or where Jesus will get the living water, or even where He comes from Himself, but the evidence will pile up for us as the excitement mounts. But for now let us rest with the conclusion of the early Church as it meditated on the mysteries of salvation: God had kept His best plan of salvation, His greatest favours and His most exalted revelations to the coming of His Son among us. He had answered the prayers of the saints of old beyond all expectation, so that we all exclaim with St Paul, in Ephesians 3:21, that God can do and has done infinitely more than we ever asked of Him or imagined that He would do, in Jesus.

The result of this miracle is that Jesus revealed His glory, and his disciples believed in Him. To reveal His glory means that Jesus gave an outward manifestation of the presence and power of God in such a way that His disciples could understand and put their faith in Him. Every true prophet had to have proper credentials. Jesus has now produced His first sign, and His disciples recognize its meaning: He is the long-awaited Messiah who will fulfil the Scriptures and give the Father's promise to all mankind, namely the overflowing gift of the Spirit (Joel 3:1–5). Later we shall be able to connect this gift with the overflowing gift of bread as John's marvellous way of presenting the Eucharistic miracle by which Jesus will feed His disciples. After His stay at Cana Jesus went down to Capernaum with His earthly and heavenly families together, and rested a few days.

The New Temple (2:13–25)

The time for the Jewish Passover was near so Jesus went up

to the Temple in Jerusalem to celebrate the feast. He went to the city that was dominated by the House of God, which is the centre of Judaism, the place of worship. One might expect that He would be received well here, but sadly we shall find that people prefer the old wine. They are used to it and they find it good. Because of this they are completely suspicious of the new wine being offered by Jesus. Here He will meet with his greatest challenges and greatest opposition. Here He will be condemned to death for just being what He is, the Son of God. And this in a city where everyone is a son of God through the Covenant! The Word will be rejected by those to whom the Word of God was given under the Old Covenant, and here lies the tragedy, and a great mystery.

At the time of Jesus the Temple of Jerusalem was a complex structure, with the Court of the Gentiles at its outermost rim. It was surrounded by very high walls, preventing any uncircumcised person from entering the inner courts of the sacred precinct, at peril of their lives. It was the only place in Israel where the Gentiles could approach God for worship. Gradually the custom began whereby the priests would refuse to accept the sacrificial animals brought by the people from their farms, demanding that they buy the animals that had been reared specially for the Temple. This gave rise to the Court of the Gentiles being used to buy and sell these animals. Since the people came from all over the Middle East they needed their foreign currency changed also, to make their purchases. Very soon no one could pray in this section of the Temple, and the Gentiles were effectively excluded from worship.

The Court of the Women of Israel (also called the treasury) was situated inside the Court of the Gentiles, then the Court of the Men. The Holy Place where the priests offered sacrifice was next, and the innermost chamber was the Holy of Holies, the place for the Ark of the Covenant, which was long since lost without trace.

Here the Presence of God manifested Itself, and only the High Priest could go into it once a year on the Day of Atonement, and even then just for a few minutes. The structure of this Temple effectively organized everyone *away* from the Presence of God. It made access to God impossible in any real sense.

Jesus was about to do two things. One was to release the position of the Gentiles and make access to God available to all peoples. He was not just the Jewish Messiah. He was the Saviour of all the world, as He will reveal in 4:42. Second, He was about to release the Temple itself, so that when the people could not come to God, God came to them. In the New Age the Temple will be invisible, lodged in the Body of Believers, who form a part of Jesus Himself, who *is the Temple of God*, carrying the fullness of God's Presence in Himself. It is through Him, with Him and in Him that all worship will go to the Father, and all response from the Father will come to us. Access is made possible for everyone, not just for those who are special. (The Letter to the Hebrews deals with this theme in detail.)

Jesus decided on drastic action, made a whip out of cord, and began a stampede of the animals as He drove them all out of the Temple. And of course the animals knocked the money changers' tables over, creating chaos. Above the din Jesus' voice rang out: "*Take all of this out of here and stop using my Father's house as a market.*" I wonder if He used the whip on the innocent animals only and not on the guilty men?

In the cleansing of the Temple Jesus showed that He was the fulfilment of many prophecies regarding the Temple. Malachi (3:1) had warned the people that God would send a messenger to prepare His way, and then the Lord whom they were expecting would suddenly come to His Temple to deal with the abuses in worship. Jeremiah (7:11–15) had already accused the priests of turning the Temple into a house of bandits. Zechariah (14:21) looked forward to the great Day of the Lord when there would be no more traders in the Temple; and Isaiah (56:7) promised that foreigners would, one day, be invited to the holy mountain and made joyful in this House of Prayer, for the house of God was a house of prayer for all peoples. There is no doubt that these prophecies were well known to the people, just as the corruption of the priestly house of Annas was! This action of Jesus was, therefore, a prophetic action in line with all the great prophets who had gone before Him, who felt the need to speak by signs, when human language fell short of communication.

The disciples did not understand the full import of the situation until after the resurrection, when they realized that Jesus had fulfilled Psalm 69:9, concerning His zeal for the house of God. The religious authorities were not impressed, however, and demanded a sign to show that He had authority to act thus. John usually refers to "The Jews" in a hostile way when he is speaking about the leaders. He wants to emphasize their implacable opposition to Jesus. They will refuse to accept any sign that He gives them, including the one he gives now concerning the resurrection. "*Destroy this Temple, and in three days I will raise it up*", He said. This is the typical enigmatic language that John uses when he wants us to read the message on two levels.

There was an expectation that the Messiah would rebuild the Temple in a very short space of time (see Hosea 6:2), so Jesus' promise would be read by His audience as a claim to be the Messiah, the one who will give them this new Temple, as we see in His trial as recounted in the Synoptics (Mark 14:58–61). But the very same words give us a message on the higher level, where Jesus promises the New Temple after His resurrection from the dead. The disciples realized this only in its fulfilment, as we are told here, and it helped them to believe more deeply in the scriptural prophecies concerning Jesus. The Temple of stone could be sullied again, but the New Temple is pure and holy, fit for

God's dwelling place. It is also the place for believers to meet God and be purified there. This indestructible Temple will be opened on the cross. By the time the gospel was written, the Jerusalem Temple was destroyed, and the Mystical Body of Christ was already in being (circa AD 90–95).

During His stay for Passover many came to believe in Him because of the signs that He worked, but as we shall see as we go along, Jesus did not accept such superficial faith. Faith must be *in Him*, not in the signs. Faith that needs signs will never mature and will always demand more signs. Faith in the person of Jesus will make real disciples. Jesus knew human nature too well to be impressed by such enthusiasm.

Chapter 3
The Bridegroom of Israel

The New Birth (3:1–12)

Nicodemus, a member of the great Sanhedrin, and, therefore, a ruler of Israel, visited Jesus by night. We have already been prepared for Nicodemus' problem in the comment at the end of the last chapter (2:23–25) that the people in Jerusalem believed on the basis of the signs worked by Jesus there, even though John has not given us any examples. Real faith in Jesus was exhibited by Mary and the disciples at Cana, so the partial faith of Nicodemus will be recognized here. He represents the partial response that Jerusalem and "officialdom" gave to Jesus, refusing to go beyond the signs to the mystery of His person. Night, for John, speaks of darkness and evil. That Nicodemus would come to Jesus by night indicated his own need to journey from darkness to the light of Christ.

Nicodemus came to Jesus full of religion. What a shock when he was calmly told that he must be born again, because to be a son of Abraham was not enough (8:53). One of the hardest concepts for people to grasp is the difference between religion and spirituality. Nicodemus must differentiate between the Law and the spirit if he is to understand even the language of Jesus, which remains on the level of the spirit. Religion was not the issue for him, he had plenty of that. It was life in the Spirit, life on the level where God can intervene in our lives daily to guide and transform us, and then use us as His instruments.

Nicodemus, being full of religion, and a teacher of the law, with its clear-cut precepts, did not realize his own arrogance and self-complacency. He spoke to Jesus from his own powerful ecclesiastical stance, with the authority of the Sanhedrin behind him. He was willing to accept Jesus as a teacher on the strength of His signs, because, he said, "*No one could perform the signs that you do unless God were with him*". This falls short of the reality of who Jesus is, for God is "*with Him*" in a unique way.

Jesus cut him short, for He has come down from "above" to invite people into a new relationship with God. If Nicodemus wants to join the Kingdom of God he will have to enter it in the same way as the other disciples. He will have to be born of God. Just as you enter human life because your earthly father begot you, so you may only enter this new heavenly life if the Father in heaven begets you. It is so simple. You must become a child of God, and Jesus alone has the power from God to make you such (1:12, 3:21).

Nicodemus is perplexed. He is listening to Jesus from the level of "below" while all the time Jesus speaks to him on the spiritual plane. This is a Johannine device used throughout the gospel which gives Jesus an opportunity to explain Himself more deeply as the conversation ensues. Nicodemus wants to know how it is possible for someone who is already alive – speaking in the human sense – to be born again? Jesus, speaking on the level of the Spirit, tells him that no one can enter the Kingdom of God unless he has passed through the "womb" of the Spirit. Only the Holy Spirit can effect this transformation, and this He does through the Baptism of Water and the Spirit (1:33). Human nature and human actions cannot effect this miracle, it is an action of God Himself. It brings with it a new relationship with God through Jesus whereby the individual becomes a Son of God, with all the privileges that this entails. Jesus wants "beloved sons" to make up the New Israel, the New People of God that He is in the process of forming.

Being a teacher of Israel, Nicodemus should have

understood that the Nation of Israel under the Old Covenant was considered to be God's first-born son (see Exodus 4:23; Hosea 11:1). With the establishment of the Davidic dynasty, the anointed king was also considered to be God's son in a special relationship to Him (see 2 Samuel 7:14). Yet the birth into the Covenant People was by a physical operation, namely circumcision, and this would be the only "spiritual rebirth" that Nicodemus knew about, apart from the new life communicated to God's people through their living of God's Word, which was understood to impart life. (See Psalm 119 where the request "by your Word give me life" is repeated twelve times; also Jeremiah 31:31–34; Ezekiel 36:26–27.)

Jesus expects him to make the transition from the old to the new as easily as Mary did at Cana. Mary succeeded where Nicodemus failed. When this conversation ends we are left with the distinct feeling that Nicodemus has not moved at all, that he is as puzzled as ever. He seems to stay in the non-decision group with regard to Jesus, which is represented by the Jewish leaders. What was so new in the teaching of Jesus was, that what was given to the nation as a whole in the Old Testament was now to be given to each individual. And it was to be given in a way that surpassed the privileges of even the greatest of the people under the former Covenant, so that the least in the Kingdom of Heaven would be greater than John the Baptist, who is the last of the Old Testament Prophets (Luke 7:29).

The difference between the old and the new is that of "flesh" and spirit, namely, what mankind can make of themselves by their own efforts, and what Jesus can do for them by means of the Spirit. Without the help of the Spirit Nicodemus is unable to comprehend. The gift of understanding flows from the Spirit of God through Jesus. If Nicodemus does not ask for the gift, he will be left outside, not because Jesus does not want to give it – that is the very reason why He came – but because we are free to choose.

Do not be surprised when I say: "*You must be born from above*". *The wind blows where it pleases . . . so it is with everyone who is born of the Spirit.* There is a mystery attached to this work of the Spirit which cannot be explained, but only experienced. The effects of the coming of the Spirit into a person's life are obvious, but no one can observe His arrival or departure, as with the wind, which Jesus uses to explain the mystery. God's Presence is invisible, but the fruits of His Presence can be clearly seen, as on Pentecost day (Acts 2). The other aspect of the mystery is why one person accepts this gift from God and another does not. Later we will see that there is a parallel here with the mysterious "coming" among them and the "departure" of Jesus which they will be unable to explain either (7:35). The Spirit who is being offered is the Spirit of Jesus (Acts 16:7), and both Jesus and the Spirit come from "above", and can hardly be understood by people who are from "below".

Nicodemus asked a question which must now be answered: How will this great thing come about? The full answer can only be given if he allows Jesus to open his blind eyes to the true origins of Jesus from "above". Only then will he acquire the heavenly perspective on things, and understand that this new relationship with God is not only possible but is being offered by Jesus now. Jesus must pay a high price for giving us this privilege, as we will see in His Hour. He must be lifted up on the cross first before the great gift of the Spirit can be poured out on thirsty people. But first Jesus chides Nicodemus for not understanding the matters we have been discussing which have their foundation in the Scriptures – and he a teacher! "*In all truth I tell you, we speak only about what we know and witness only to what we have seen and yet you people reject our evidence.*" Nicodemus had come to Jesus with a heavy ecclesiastical "We know . . . " Now Jesus picks him up on it, and says that He speaks only what *He knows* and witnesses only to what He has seen, but He uses the plural "we know" thus associating Himself with the Father, from whom He came. Nicodemus is among the group who did not accept Jesus' evidence. Nicodemus disappears from the scene here but will reappear in the passion, and Jesus addresses Himself to "you people" (verse 11) who are represented by him.

The mention of evidence shows that this first half of this gospel is one vast trial for the Beloved Son, in which He bears witness to the Father first before the people of Israel, then before the authorities, and finally before the world, through Pilate. In the second half we will see Jesus prepare His beloved disciples for the fact that after the resurrection the new Community will be on trial before the world for the whole of its existence, and they must bear witness to Jesus, through the power of the Spirit, just as he had borne witness to the Father.

Jesus is unique as a witness to the Father because He has been in heaven. He is the only one who has seen God (1:18), and can therefore speak for Him. Nevertheless, the New Birth will only be given when Jesus has been lifted up on the cross first and then in glory, which fact is unacceptable to the Jews. His Hour initiates His Ascent to heaven, which reverses the descent from heaven and proves it conclusively. The Word who had become flesh would return to where He came from in the Father's bosom. This return to the Father would be proof of His claim to be the great "I AM" later also. In this way John reminds us of the Suffering Servant who suffered before being exalted on high (Isaiah 52–53).

There is a clue for us in Moses' action in the desert when he lifted up the bronze serpent as a *sign* for the people who were in need of healing, that if they looked to this sign with faith they would be healed (Numbers 21:4–9). . . . *as Moses lifted up the snake in the desert, so must the Son of man be lifted up so that everyone who believes may have eternal life in Him.* The Book of Wisdom (16:6–17) says that it was a sign of salvation, enabling them to look to God, as Saviour, for their healing. The sign given to Israel now is the cross of Jesus, the most unwelcome sign that God could choose (1 Corinthians 1:23), because the sign of "the cross" was as much a symbol of the curse of sin as the serpent was. They must penetrate the mystery of the cross if they are to understand the gift of Salvation offered to them in Jesus. It is the mystery of Incarnate Love, battered and bruised to bring forth the New Wine of the Kingdom of God.

The issue in the sign of the Son of Man is eternal life – that quality of living at the highest level of our being, here and now, in this present life, and then having the happiness of heaven too. Jesus raises us to His level of being, to operate by His principles and to produce the same divine fruit. This is the gift He gives to anyone who believes in Him. Jesus does not want onlookers in His Community, but participators: not theorists but those who will live the same life as Himself.

For this is how God loved the world: He gave His only son, so that everyone who believes in Him may not perish but may have eternal life. This gift is a manifestation of God's love for us, not of judgement, as everyone had expected for the great Day of the Lord's visitation. God's love was not directed at some élite group of holy people but to the cosmos, *the unbelieving world* who were not friends of God. So this love of God is completely unmerited on our part, a gift from His heart, through His Beloved Son.

If Jesus really is God's Son from "above", why do so many reject Him? How could they reject the mystery of God Incarnate? John begins to answer this unspoken objection of the Jews now. Like an X-ray which shows up everything that is exposed to it, the Son entered the world, and showed up those who were disposed to receive God's love and those who were not, simply by their response to

Him. Those who reject the Beloved Son put themselves outside of the Salvation offered by the Lord, and so "judge" themselves. They did not realize that God's X-ray had been on them, showing up their unbelief and their sinful ways. The coming of Jesus forces the moment of decision upon us, and some *prefer* the darkness they are in to the possibility of a new life. John adds that the reason for this is their attachment to sin: they love their sin. *And the judgement is this: though the light has come into the world people have preferred darkness to the light because their deeds were evil.* For John the real sin, that which underlies all other sins, is unbelief, the refusal to accept Jesus and the new life He offers.

And the X-ray shows up something else: *By their fruits you will know them* we read in the synoptics (Matthew 7:20). Here John tells us that it is not believing "in the head" that counts but *doing the works* of the New Life. People who continue in sin show that they are still in darkness, but those who live by the new Love Jesus is introducing will demonstrate that they have entered the New Life, and they will experience its transforming power as they live it.

The Bridegroom is Revealed (3:22–36)

John the Baptist now appears for the last time in this gospel. His exit is fitting for one whom Jesus declared was the greatest born of woman (Matthew 11:11). His final witness to Jesus makes it clear that Jesus is the Bridegroom of Israel, and that the New People of God are the New Bride in formation. There will be a marriage "on the third day"! And this marriage will reveal the New Wine of the Kingdom of God.

After this Jesus went from Jerusalem into the countryside of Judaea with His disciples and began to baptize. This was not Christian Baptism, which was dependent on Jesus being glorified after His Hour. It meant that Jesus took up His work where John left off, as more people needed to be prepared for the grace to come. JB was still baptizing at the time, at Aenon. Some identify Aenon with the springs in the Jordan valley, while others would claim a place in Samaria. It was just before JB had been arrested. During a discussion between JB's disciples and a Jew over purification rites, JB was told that Jesus was baptizing too. This is a very simple setting for the close of one ministry and the opening of another, where the disciples are confused and ask for clarification. It also deals with the difference between the Baptism of the new order and the rites of the old. Anyone drinking the old wine will not be interested in the new, except perhaps as a point for theological debate.

It is the bridegroom who has the bride; and yet the bridgroom's friend, who stands there and listens to him, is filled with joy at the bridegroom's voice. This joy I now feel, and it is complete. But let us remember the two levels the gospel is speaking on. John the Baptist is from earth, from "below", while Jesus is from heaven, from "above", so JB repeats his testimony that he is not the Christ, and can claim only the grace given to him. Jesus can claim what heaven has given to Him also. The I AM NOT is the one to point out the I AM. JB, who comes from the old order, uses Israel's own language regarding the relationship between God and His people, to point out that Jesus is the legitimate Bridegroom, just as the Father had revealed Himself to be in the Old Testament. JB himself was only the best man, the one whose function it was to prepare the bride for her husband, and to present her as a true virgin on her wedding day (2 Corinthians 11:2). He is full of joy that his function is complete, and as the lesser, he gives way before the greater. In JB the Old Testament surrenders gracefully to the New: the water gives way before the wine.

John the evangelist has been showing us how Jesus was to replace the Temple and all its observances. (Was there a statement about animal sacrifices, in Jesus driving the animals out of the Temple, thus setting them free to live out their normal existence?) He was to replace Nicodemus' sense-bound religion with something completely spiritual. Now here we are shown that Christian Baptism will replace the old purificatory rites. The old must surrender to the new with the gracefulness and humility of John the Baptist.

In a final reflection, the evangelist summarizes some of the ideas in this chapter to make sure that his readers have seen the implications of what was said. Jesus is the "one who comes", therefore the Messiah. He is not only Messiah, but the unique revealer of God because He comes from "above", and takes precedence over all others. Yet the mystery is that His testimony is not accepted generally, though anyone who does not accept it testifies to the truth of God. The great prophets before Christ – including John the Baptist – were given a measure of God's Spirit to carry out their mission. Jesus is utterly unique in possessing the fullness of the Spirit of God . . . *for God gives Him the Spirit without reserve.* Therefore it is He who brings the definitive revelation of God to us. In an outpouring of Love, God entrusted everything to Jesus, so it is only through Him that we receive God's Word and God's Salvation. No one else will be coming after the Beloved Son. He is God's greatest gift to humanity, and since Jesus alone possesses the fullness of the Spirit, He alone can impart Him to us, after His Hour.

Finally, anyone who believes in the Son is given the gift of Eternal Life, but anyone who refuses this gift will never "see" life, meaning that they will never experience this new life in the spirit being offered by Jesus, the only Saviour. This leaves them exposed to God's justice, a thing which no sinner can afford.

Chapter 4
The New Life

As we set out with Jesus for Samaria we must remember an important factor in John, that in order to understand the material he is about to present we must be conscious of all that has gone before. We must carry over from the previous chapters the insights that enable us to interpret this one. This is because John is in the process of building up evidence about Jesus as he allows his gospel to unfold, and he does so much like waves breaking on a shore one after the other in sequence.

Thus far Jesus has revealed Himself only to Jews, and with mixed results. Some have accepted Him as the Messiah and become His disciples. Others are impressed by His signs, but no more, for they fail to penetrate the mystery of His person. Those who remain uncommitted and on the sideline because they do not accept His claims, will soon become hostile.

Now John turns his attention to those outside of Judaism, first to the Samaritans and then to the Gentiles who lived in the land, as the court official at the end of this chapter probably was. Unlike Nicodemus and the Jews, these people are not properly "born" into the people of God. They have little or no access to the Word of God, and so their knowledge of God is incomplete and imperfect. The Samaritans held that only the Books of Moses were inspired, whereas "properly born" sons of Abraham, like Nicodemus, had access to the whole of the Old Testament scriptures. Nicodemus also had the edge in being able to worship at the "proper" Temple in Jerusalem, whereas the Samaritans had to settle for Mount Gerizim, and the

Gentiles had to accept the crumbs that fell from the Jewish table, as we observed in the cleansing of the Temple (Mark 7:28).

The question is raised in our minds then as to whether these deprived people are at a disadvantage with regard to Jesus and the new Life that He offers. Strangely, we find that it is the Jews, represented by the response of Nicodemus , who fail to grasp His gift. The Samaritan woman and the court official come to conclusions, not from an official stance of accepted theology, but from personal experience of Jesus. They come openly and honestly, and struggle to freedom with His help. Nicodemus, on the other hand, is handicapped by his "advantages", as the Apostle Paul later confessed himself to be when he began to consider all these assets as disadvantages! (Philippians 3:7).

As we have seen in the last chapter, Jesus alone can provide the only birth that matters. He is God's *Word*, and Wisdom Incarnate, the one who provides true knowledge of God. He is also the New Temple, where the Spirit of God rests, the place where God is to be encountered, where access to God is available to all, and where our petitions to God are "processed". He alone can give the gift of the Spirit. All of this becomes a reality with Jesus' Hour. Here John plunges us into a new set of images if we are not already overcome by the rich food we have had. He will now compare two "waters": the flat water of the cistern and the bubbling water of the deep well which tasted much better. The old order is "flat and stale" whereas the New Life is "bubbling up to eternal life". Again you must make your choice as to which water you choose.

Living water is a symbol used throughout the Old Testament for God's Wisdom found in the scriptures, a wisdom that imparts life to us (see Proverbs 13:14). Proverbs calls God's word a "life-giving fountain". Isaiah (55:1) invites all who are thirsty to come to the water, and Sirach comes very close to Jesus' words here in saying that "anyone who eats me will hunger for more, and anyone who drinks me will thirst for more". Jesus is about to offer a living water to quench all thirst, so it surpasses the gift of the Old Order. The Torah was the most important part of the Old Testament, considered by the people to be more inspired than the rest, so we find Sirach (24:23–29) singing the praises of the Torah, that it makes wisdom overflow in a person's life like a fountain of living water.

The term "living water" also denotes the gift of the Spirit to be given by Jesus. He was in the process of building up a community of Spirit-filled people who would dispense the life-giving waters of God's Word and God's grace to the needy world. As we have already seen, Jesus connects "water" and the "Spirit", just as in the Old Testament we find them associated (7:37–39).

The Samaritan Woman (4:1–26)

When the Pharisees heard that Jesus and His disciples were baptizing and making more disciples than JB, it spelt trouble. It was most likely just after JB's arrest, and so it would be dangerous for Jesus to appear to continue His ministry. He left Judaea for the more friendly Galilee, and we never again hear any reference to Him baptizing. Instead He concentrates on preaching the Word and giving signs of God's Presence. He decided to visit Samaria on the way to Galilee, even though he could have travelled a different road. The fact that John tells us that Jesus "had to pass through Samaria" has more to do with his Father's will, than to geographical necessity.

On the way he came to a Samaritan town called Sychar near the land that Jacob gave to his son Joseph. This is most likely the Shechem of Genesis 33:18, where the well is only a very short distance from the town. Here, instead of the spiritual blindness of night that we had with Nicodemus, we will encounter spiritual awakening in broad daylight. Jesus identifies with the spiritual sources of Israel in Jacob the Founder-Father, and Joseph her first saviour. He sat down by the well because He was tired – how often we have met with such incidents before! (Genesis 24:11–17 for Abraham and Rebecca; 29:1–21 for Jacob and Rachel; Exodus 2:15–21 for Moses and Seporah). Each one of these meetings was a divine appointment between a chosen man of God and a woman who would be associated with him in his mission. The presence of Seporah, an outsider and a foreigner (as was Joseph's wife), should prepare us for the surprise of the Samaritan woman.

The well was about a hundred feet deep, and the water it continues to give two thousand years later still looks like *living water*. As Jesus sat down He would be aware of Himself as the New Well, the source of divine life for everyone in need. It was midday, which signifies that we are about to see the full glory of revelation, a fact that puts Jesus in a different category to Jacob, who had only the pale light of a distant past. The sun is at its zenith as Jesus, the Saviour of all the world, begins to reveal Himself, not only to a woman, but to a Samaritan! What is God saying to us in this about our prejudices and our categorizing of people according to sex, race and social position? Is it not an illustration of the fact that His thoughts are as different from ours as the heavens are from the earth? (Isaiah 55:8–9).

A Samaritan woman then came to draw water. This chore was normally done in the early morning, and the women usually went together for safety, but this woman is alone. Did she come because she saw Jesus there? We will discover she has had a poor history in personal relationships. Does she view Jesus as another possibility? If so she is cured the moment He speaks, for she exclaims in disgust that he is a Jew! Might we not see here that it is not our motivation in coming to Jesus that God cares about, but just the fact that we come. Jesus can deal with the situation.

This woman has nothing but disadvantages on her side. She is a half-Jew. Her ancestors intermarried with the Assyrian conquerors of the Northern Kingdom a long time ago. This is seen as an allusion to the five husbands later, as there were five nationalities involved, all of whom worshipped their own gods but also adopted the true God, the real Bridegroom of Israel (2 Kings 17:24–41). In Jewish eyes, therefore, she is both a heretic and unclean. Then she was a woman! Men in those days did not consider women capable of participating in theological debates. They regarded them as having inferior intellects, and generally as lesser beings than men. Jesus cut through these conventions and the laws of ritual impurity, and spoke to this woman with respect, as a child of God, and also as a person of dignity in her own right, capable of coming to her own conclusions. His attitude liberated her, not just spiritually but socially. As she had embodied the troubles of Samaria in her own person, Jesus made her the first Christian missionary to Samaria.

Salvation is God's gift to us, and comes on His initiative, so Jesus opened the dialogue with a request that the woman give him a drink of her water, even though He has come to give her living water! The humility of the Incarnate Son should not be missed here, nor his respect before a child of God. This woman is thirsty for God in her life, as she will discover, and Jesus is thirsty for God's Salvation to be accomplished. The next time we hear of His thirst will be on the cross – also at the sixth hour (19:14), when he will accomplish the salvation He now offers.

The ensuing conversation follows the usual pattern in John, with the woman misunderstanding Jesus because she stays on the level of "below", whereas He speaks on the spiritual level. Gradually He will bring her up to His level where she can participate in the New Life that He offers.

If you only knew what GOD is offering and who it is that is saying to you,"Give me a drink", you would have been the one to ask, and He would give you living water. There are two challenges here: one to penetrate the mystery of His person, and the other to ask for the New Life, both of which go together. If the woman can now look deeply enough into Jesus' eyes, she will find God. What a far cry from what her faulty motivation would have led her to! She has now the same privilege as Moses had, when God revealed Himself to him as if he were the only person that existed – and she a woman, and a Samaritan! She, who could not enter the inner precincts of the Temple, now finds God out here at the well. And this is how it will be in the future, as Jesus tells her that not only is Mount Gerizim obsolete, but also Mount Zion! God wants those who will worship Him in spirit and in truth, and that can be done anywhere. It requires no building as Jesus is the "Temple", the locus of God's presence for us.

The woman responds to Jesus respectfully, calling Him *Kyrie*, which can be translated both as "sir" and "Lord". John most likely expects us to read it as a progression in her faith as she comes closer to the truth she is about to embrace. Since Jesus has no bucket she asks: "*How do you get this living water?*" While she asks this on the material level, she unconsciously asks the right question, and Jesus will respond to the deepest level of meaning that the words convey. Already on the way now, she suspects that He may be greater than Jacob, though not comprehending *from where* this water comes, just as the president of the marriage feast did not know where the new wine had come from either. But we who watch this drama unfold, *we know*, and that is the important thing. A flashback to 1:51 reminds us that Jesus claimed to be a greater sign than Jacob's ladder. His "water" is greater than Jacob's too, which will leave us needing more, whereas Jesus' Living Water will not only quench all thirst, but also become an endless supply inside us, bubbling up to eternal life.

What the woman thirsts for is a meaningful knowledge of

and relationship with God, and she can find this in Jesus sitting before her, but her faith-level must grow before this can happen. Yet she asks for His gift: she risks accepting His offer, even though she interprets it on the wrong level, saying that it will only stop her from coming to *this well*. Again she has unconsciously stumbled on the truth, for it *is* a new spiritual life that is being offered that will free her from her sinful past, and from the need to offer animal sacrifice to a God she does not really know even though she worships Him.

"*Go and call your husband,*" *Jesus said to her*, "*and come back here.*" *The woman answered*, "*I have no husband.*" *Jesus said to her*, "*You are right . . . for although you have had five, the one you now have is not your husband.*" Calling her into deeper truth, Jesus asks her to "make room" for God in her life, and as He does so reveals His identity "from above". She must go and bring back her husband. It sounds so simple, but she has had five husbands, and so she avoids the moving-in on her moral life, by refusing to admit she was living with anyone. She must come to acknowledge that her behaviour expresses her real life, what she really is, and that religion without morality is monstrous. The doctrine and the life must be one. He is taking her seriously in making this request. Jesus reveals His supernatural knowledge of her life and her failed attempts at marriage.

In asking the question Jesus managed to extract the truth from her, that her present companion could not be called a "husband". How gentle He is in calling forth a confession from us! The woman realized that Jesus must be a prophet, and her address of "Sir" could now be read "Lord", showing her growth in knowledge. Her chaotic personal life does not surprise or shock Jesus, but He wants to deal with it. This woman must allow the water of her life to be transformed into the wine of the New Life: or, to stay in the present metaphor, her stale water must be replaced by His bubbling new water.

The Samaritans were expecting a prophet-like-Moses to come to them (Deuteronomy 18:15–18), so Jesus speaks to her as that person, but goes on to the full revelation of Himself as Messiah. The coming prophet was expected to settle disputes over worship, particularly over the question of which mountain was the right one, Jerusalem or Gerizim, so the woman broaches the subject, only to discover that they are worshipping, not only on the wrong mountain but on the wrong level! It is the spiritual reality, not the physical, that interests God in worship. He is giving them the worship "from above" and they must let go what they had "from below".

The Holy Spirit will guide the worship of the community Jesus is founding, and it will be based on His revealed truth. This community will worship God *as Father* and this can be done only by His children who possess His spirit (Romans 8:15–16). Through the Spirit they will be able to enter the indestructible Temple that is Jesus, and there encounter God, for He is truly present in Jesus as Jesus is in the Spirit. The Spirit raises us above the level of the flesh, thus enabling us to worship God properly. Here Jesus is fulfilling the revelation about the Moses-like-prophet who would explain everything to them. Although He has come for all peoples, yet God sent this revelation through the Jews, and Salvation happens in and through Jesus who is a Jew. This we must all accept. But what He offers transcends Judaism since He is "from above", and His gift is to Jew and Gentile alike. Through Jesus everyone is offered the privilege of coming to God as our *real Father*, to be loved and cared for as His *real family*, those whom He has begotten through the Spirit.

The moment of full truth has arrived as the woman wonders whether the prophet they are expecting could be the Messiah. Jesus reveals that He transcends the expectations of Jews and Samaritans by revealing Himself with the exact same words which God used to identify Himself to

Moses: *EGO EIMI* (Exodus 3:14). Jesus is, therefore, the true Son of Moses' God, and the definitive revealer of God. The heavenly I AM can now be encountered in the Incarnate I AM here at the well. That revelation, fit for Moses himself, was given to the most unlikely recipient. The meeting of the "I AM NOT" of the sinner and the I AM of the Saviour is a wonderful revelation of God's unfathomable Love. The I AM in dialogue with the sinner means healing and hope for a fallen world. When we could not come to Him, He came to us.

Dialogue with the Disciples (4:27–42)

On arrival back from the town where they had gone to buy food for the lunch, the disciples were shocked to find Jesus speaking to a woman. This was flouting convention, but they did not dare ask Him what He wanted from her. Not even Jesus is credited with pure motives! Their thinking is "from below", so He will have to draw them back to His level if they are to participate in the harvest He is about to reap. It seems they are unaware that He is the Saviour of all the world, but they will learn this from the Samaritans whom, as Jews, they despised.

The woman, meanwhile, left her water-jar at the feet of Jesus and ran back to the town, hardly aware that she will never be the same again. She has forgotten the reason why she went to the well in the first place. Without her realizing it, He has already quenched her thirst, so the water-jar symbolizes the laying down of the old life before Jesus. As she ran off in faith, He had the freedom to transform her into a true disciple who will now proclaim His Word effectively to the whole town. Who, but the Beloved Son, who had been in the Bosom of the Father for all eternity, could have known that this poor sinner held the key to Samaria?

By contrast the disciples judged Jesus on the "flesh-level", and could not understand why He was no longer hungry. His deep "thirst" for the salvation of sinners was being quenched at that moment too, as he saw the harvest from Samaria begin to come towards Him. The woman was about to offer Jesus the only food that could truly satisfy Him. Or to round off their conversation, she gives him the drink He asked her for, and He gives her the well from which she and her people will find life.

The woman extended the correct invitation to her people, that they should come and experience Jesus for themselves, and hear His living word. There is no mention of signs and wonders. They are invited to meet the one who reads hearts and renews lives.

How different from the miracle-hungry crowds in Jerusalem! No wonder Jesus felt refreshed. These people were coming to real faith. This is an object lesson for the disciples, who will, after the death and resurrection of Jesus, have to reap the harvest He had sown in Samaria (Acts 8: 4–25). The prophets had foretold that the days of Messiah would make the mountains overflow with new wine and give bumper harvests, where there would be overlapping of sowing and reaping (Amos 9:13; Leviticus 26:5; Psalm 126:5–6).

Jesus is sowing the seed that the beloved disciples will reap. The seed has been drenched with the "tears" of His martyrdom to make it life-giving for all time. They, in their turn, will not only reap His harvest but will go on to sow seed for the next generation, who in turn will reap theirs. They too will be called upon to drench the seed with the tears of their repentance first, and later of their martyrdom, and so the sower and reaper will rejoice together. What they see here in Samaria must be taken to the ends of the earth.

This woman is an example for the disciples, showing as she does that Jesus can be found by unbelievers through the words of the truly converted person. This was to be the pattern for their future mission to all the world, where each new generation would hear the message through those converted sinners who were now His missionaries. So true was the woman's testimony that the townspeople came out looking for Jesus Himself. They will be satisfied only with the fullness of truth, so they invite Him to stay with them, something unheard of for a Jew to do.

The disciples will have to work out this problem of staying with the "unclean" after Jesus' death (Acts 10:15–16). Two days of "I AM " staying with them, and the whole town came to the momentous conclusion, on the third day, that God was with them. The "I AM" was the Saviour of all the world. This was the spiritual resurrection of Samaria. The mission is declared to be universal. Their faith has matured, and no longer rests on the frail testimony of a recently converted sinner. It rests instead on the word of Jesus Himself, the only foundation of truth.

The Second Cana Miracle (4:43–54)

After two days, Jesus left for Galilee, arriving in Cana again "on the third day". The Galileans received Him well, but for the same reason as the crowds in Jerusalem: they were impressed by His miracles. Jesus did not consider this a great honour to Him, as this type of faith is very inadequate and incomplete, failing as it does to see beyond the miracle to what it signifies. They were willing to see His works, but would not listen to His Word or put their faith in Him. John shows that the Jews in general gave this inadequate response to Jesus, a fact that culminated in His death later.

Jesus inaugurated the New Age in Cana on his previous visit. Now He will show his power over life and death, and the characters in this drama will be a "royal father" and his "son who is about to die". Thus John prepares us for the revelation of the relationship between Jesus and His Father in the next chapter, where the price of Jesus giving the new Life will be that He will have to die, as He told Nicodemus (3:14).

The court official who approached Jesus was most likely from the household of Herod Antipas, the Tetrarch of Galilee, and was probably a Gentile. (This healing has close parallels with the healing of the Centurion's son in the Synoptics, Matthew 8:5–13; Luke 7:1–10.) He travelled twenty miles to meet Jesus because his little boy was dying, only to find Jesus very unsympathetic toward him. It is important to see that Jesus speaks to him in the plural "you", not in the singular. This indicates that this man is being treated as the representative of the Galilean crowds, just as the woman of Samaria was of her people, and Nicodemus of Jerusalem.

If he has genuinely come to seek life for his son, this man cannot afford to get caught on "signs and wonders". His faith will have to go beyond that, if Jesus is to be allowed to give what He has in Himself for this boy. Jesus, as we have seen, is the source of life, but only a true faith in Him can release this gift into a person's life. And it can only be received by a heart that is open to the truth that Jesus offers, as we have observed in the last chapter. The overflowing gift of life that Jesus gives is indeed a wonder, but not in the sense of something that dazzles and stuns, while not transforming lives. His gift opens blind eyes to the wonder of true faith, and enables the recipient to walk a new path in life. Jesus will not accept a miracle that merely solves a material problem while leaving the person still in the blindness of unbelief, and, therefore, outside the Kingdom of God. That would negate the reason for His coming.

"*Sir* (kyrie), *come down before my child dies.*" "*Go home*", *said Jesus*, "*your son will live.*" The man did not understand Jesus but decided to trust Him nevertheless. He probably said: "Lord, come down!" His desperation for his son made him go beyond speech. Time was ticking away, and the journey home was a long one. This plea was deeper than even he knew. The whole of humanity was desperate to have someone save them from death, and from all the "dead" areas in our lives, and time was running out for us. Jesus must DO something! All humanity cries thus to Jesus through this man: Come down from where You are to where we are, and see our desperate state, feel our need, and give us Your gift of life. For that to happen, of course, Jesus the Son of the Father will have to die. It is life in exchange for life.

The challenge given to the man was that he should go home believing on the word of Jesus alone, without having seen any sign whatever. This is quite a test in the circumstances, yet he rose to the occasion. His first steps in real faith were on that journey home. Was he expecting life or death to meet him? To go home without the healer, to walk away believing; that was the sign that released the gift of life in the son to restore his physical well-being. It was obedience to the word of God that released the power of God into the situation. The man, like ourselves, discovered this only in the *doing* of the action, not in a theoretical discussion. Believers "do" the works of truth and light and thereby discover its power (3:21).

But at the same time the man discovered that he had a well of "living water" given to him that was now bubbling up to eternal life, not only for himself but for his whole household. What a sign for everyone! Already John has illustrated the kind of faith that merits the praise of Jesus: "Blessed are those who have not seen and yet believe" (20:29). And this applies also to the household who believe on the word of the man, just as Samaria had believed on the word of the woman. Again we have the future work of the beloved disciples shown. It will be their privilege to take the word of Jesus to all the needy, and release in them the gift of life, from the overflowing fountain within themselves, and the Body of Christ (7:37–39).

Samaria brought a great harvest to Jesus, so too, did this household. While still on his way home, the servants came to meet the man to tell him the good news of his son's recovery. On enquiry he found that the boy was healed at the very moment he had put his trust in Jesus. It happened at "the seventh hour", about one o'clock in the day – hardly the time when a person dangerously ill would suddenly recover. So it was obvious that God had been at work recreating life, and Jesus demonstrated His power over death. The number seven is usually used in the scriptures to denote something complete and perfect. Is John emphasizing the maturity of the father's faith, or the perfection of the harvest which followed it?

This was Jesus' second sign, given at Cana. In the first sign He began to show the "greater things" He had promised to Nathanael. Now we see the progression in this sign and the further ones by which he will reveal the Mystery of Life that exists within Himself for all. Jesus has illustrated what He taught that "everyone who believes may have eternal life" (3:15). The Samaritan woman believed, as did her townspeople. Then the official believed with all of his household. This is Jesus' "food", to do the will of the Father in bringing people to believe in Him, and it introduces the work of Father and Son in the next chapter.

Chapter 5

The Father and the Son

Chapter five continues the cycle of Jesus' signs that both point and lead to His passion and death. But there is a new emphasis. Before, the uniqueness of Jesus' Person was presented to an ever widening audience, beginning with His family, His disciples and friends; then the Jews in general; and finally the Samaritans and the Gentiles. Through it all we discovered that Jesus was not just the Jewish Messiah, but also the Saviour of all the world.

Now we find that concentration is given to the Jews, specifically those who reject Jesus and His claims. The following chapters read like a vast trial of the Son of Man before the Jewish nation, which reflects the deep conflicts between the Church of John and the Synagogue in his own day. Later (chapter 16) we will find that the community of the beloved disciples will be on trial also before the world, and they must witness to Jesus, as Jesus here witnesses to the Father. In fact the gospel *is* part of that witness.

John uses a new technique now as he presents Jesus' signs in association with specific Jewish feasts. In each case he associates the sign, the feast and the discourse by making references in the discourse to both the sign worked and the feast that occasioned it. For example: in the first sequence there are several references to the Sabbath, and what may also be a few veiled allusions to Pentecost, as he cites Moses and the Law (5:9–10). The second one, in 6:22–71, links the multiplication of the loaves with the feast of Passover and the Manna in the desert. The long discourse in 7:1–8:58 ties with Tabernacles, while the short one in 10:22–39 links with the feast of the Dedication of the

Temple. It is John's powerful way of saying that Jesus replaces all the feasts of the Jews, not by destroying them, but by fulfilling them. This is seen at the close, in the final Passover (11:55) which He fulfills in His death and glorification.

The Man on the Mat (5:1–18)

Jesus again went up to Jerusalem for a Jewish feast, which John does not name, as he wants to concentrate on Jesus working on the Sabbath, the sacred day of rest. He will weave the theme of the feast into the discourse later. Jesus went to the north of the Temple area to a pool called Bethesda, which means the House of Mercy. This was located beside the Sheep Pool, and was later found under the Church of St Anne in Jerusalem. Here Jesus chose to manifest the mercy of God to a man who was all but dead physically, emotionally and spiritually, in a sign that amounts to a virtual resurrection.

Apparently this pool was reputed to have some medicinal qualities, and the sick gathered around its five porticos to wait for the water to move each year. The story had it that an angel of the Lord visited the pool and stirred up its waters, so that whoever went in first was healed of their trouble. It seems that only one person per year was healed – a very depressing fact for the crowds in need.

This place represents the condition of everyone in the cosmos, the unbelieving world. If we look at them from the vantage point of the overflowing New Life that Jesus offers, they are sick spiritually, as well as blind, lame, paralysed and impotent, overcome by the sheer weight of living. The five porticos are a reminder of the five Books of the Law, which could point the way to life but were powerless to change anyone. This water was useless also, as it did not meet the needs of the people. There was great need for the transforming touch of Jesus, to give life both to the waters

(Baptism) and to raise the people from the dead. This would be a divine work done in tandem between the Father and the Son.

If Nicodemus encapsulated the problems of Judaism, the Samaritan woman that of half-Jews, and the court official the Gentiles, then the man whom Jesus picks out here represents the desperation of everyone under the old order, including the millions who live in quiet despair today, who have no sense of destiny or of meaning to life, who just "get through" each day, they know not how, or why. In every sense except the physical they are dead, hopeless, without even the curiosity to enquire if there is a Saviour to help. He represents those under the Old Covenant also, who found that the Law of Moses was inadequate to give life, and they had to await the "angel of the Lord" to come.

As Jesus approached the man, we the readers know that someone infinitely greater than an angel is visiting the pool. We have learned that Salvation comes from the Divine initiative (3:16), so Jesus offers new life, but will not force the free will of the person. "*Do you want to be well again*?" he asked. Becoming well involves taking up the responsibilities of the new life, and responding to the grace of the Lord. He would be expected to do the works of light and become a disciple, but then he may prefer the darkness (3:19). A transformation of life and behaviour is needed to bring about this resurrection. Jesus is calling him to the new life, but he must hear and respond (5:25).

The response was not very encouraging, as the man complained that his condition was due to the actions of others. But still he did not openly reject, and actually obeyed the command of Jesus to rise to new life. His healing was not complete though for he did not even enquire who Jesus was, let alone penetrate the mystery of His person. He was still passive and unresponsive. Yet for the people who have eyes to see, a great sign has been given: one who was known to be a write-off for thirty-eight years has received new life. But who will "see"?

Jesus disappeared into the crowd for a while, and quietly sought out this lost sheep in the Temple precincts, where the final stage of his healing would take place privately (Luke 15:4). Jesus challenged him to respond to the gift that had been given: "*Now that you are well again, do not sin any more, or something worse may happen to you.*" Jesus was not implying that he was sick because he was a sinner (9:3), but that he must turn away from the false value-system of the cosmos to co-operate with the grace given. He must learn that the egocentric stance in life is death-dealing, while the self-giving stance of love is health-giving, and we are free to choose one or the other.

It happened that that day was the Sabbath, and it was forbidden to carry beds or heavy objects around. The Jewish leaders had no eyes for a resurrection, only for the infringement of a law (Jeremiah 17:21–27). They want to know who this healer is, not to praise Him for a great work, but only to condemn Him as a Sabbath-breaker, for it was expressly forbidden to work on the Sabbath, and healing was considered to be work.

Jesus answered: "*My Father still goes on working, and I am at work, too.*" Though Genesis 2:2–4 speaks of God resting on the Sabbath, most rabbis understood that this could not be strictly so, for creation would cease if God removed His sustaining hand. God continued to give and take life on the Sabbath, as neither birth nor death respects the days of the week! He therefore gives life and pronounces judgement on the Sabbath (2 Kings 5:7). He is Lord of the Sabbath. This divine prerogative Jesus now claims to Himself, but only those with eyes to see will understand. All others will join the Jews in wanting to kill Him, now that they clearly hear Him claim God as His own Father, thus making Himself equal to God.

Father and Son (5:19–30)

The time has come to reveal the relationship that exists between the Father and the Beloved Son, who had rested on His bosom for all eternity, and who now works in tandem with Him in the re-creation of those in need of salvation. This brings us to one of the most exalted heights of John's Gospel, as we breathe the pure air of the mutuality of their self-giving love for the sake of humans who do not appreciate what is done for them.

First, the Son can do nothing by Himself. He admits that He is powerless alone. It is the Father's life and power that is being expressed through Him, and He continually looks to the Father and takes His cue from Him. He is utterly surrendered to the Father's will and carries that out. The other side of the relationship is that the Father *loves* the Son and manifests Himself fully to Him, so that the Son can imitate Him in everything. Later, in chapters 14 and 15, we shall see that this is the pattern for the relationship between Jesus and His beloved disciples.

Thus we see that the life given to the boy in the last chapter is merely a sign of the "real life" that Jesus has been empowered to give by His Father. Also the command not to sin any more, which was given to the healed cripple, becomes clearer, for sin leaves one in the realm of death. The Son has the power to call such a one to "life", and the only threat to the continuance of that life is to go on sinning. Jesus intends to do even greater works than He has done up to now. He has power to call the spiritually dead to life now, while those who are physically dead will be called in the general resurrection on the last day. Thus John combines the idea of realized eschatology, namely what happens to us in the here and now, with his future eschatology, which is the fulfilment at the end of time. The reading of this discourse is intended by John to be a gift of life to his readers in the here and now of time. If we respond to the grace offered, then, even as we read, we can receive the gift of eternal life. Why delay?

Included in the power to give life is judgement, and the Father leaves all judgement to the Son. In Psalm 82 those who judge others are called "sons of the Most High" because of their power over life and death. Since this power in its most exalted sense has been given to the Son, He should be honoured as the Father is honoured, but of course it would be unthinkable to the Jews that anyone could be honoured as the Father was. As we have seen before, the arrival of the Son automatically brings judgement in the here-and-now, as His light shows up the secret thoughts of many hearts, and discriminates between those who believe and those who reject.

But He will be the supreme judge on the Last Day too, and that will bring this mighty trial to its conclusion (3:11), when He will judge all those who refused to believe in Him or accept His free gift of grace and Salvation (Matthew 25:31–46). Jesus is the mysterious Son of Man, whom Daniel foretold would be given glory, dominion and kingship in the future age, but who would also judge the dead (Daniel 7:13, 12:2). Yet even though He has been given all this power Jesus refuses to exercise it except in total dependence on His Father. He does what the Father wants, and so His judgement is just.

Witnesses for the Son (5:31–40)

Depending on whether we look at this case from "above" or "below" will determine how we see Jesus. From the "above" position He is the judge about to show the real situation to the Jewish leaders. He presents witnesses to confirm His testimony, and in so doing shows up their obstinacy and unbelief. From "below" He is accused of blasphemy and must bring forth His defence in a trial that could culminate in His death, since blasphemy was a capital offence.

According to Deuteronomy 19:15, a man could not be convicted on the testimony of a single witness. Several were required to sustain the charge in the case of a capital offence (Numbers 35:30; Deuteronomy 17:6). As Jesus is preparing a case for the condemnation of the Jewish leaders He must not compromise Himself by witnessing on His own behalf, as this was forbidden, yet later, in 8:14, He will claim His right to do this, since no one knows His real origins except Himself.

He presents no less than four witnesses, but His "star" witness is the Father, who is invisible in this court. The others merely externalize the testimony of the Father. The first to be called to the witness stand is John the Baptist, who, because he was a "man sent by God", reflects the Father's witness. The Jewish leaders had sent a delegation to JB (1:19) who had borne witness to Jesus as the one who was to come. Jesus does not need this testimony, but He mentions it for their sake, the inference being that if they had accepted the witness of JB they would have been prepared to accept Him also. The really damning bit is that Jesus is aware that the Jewish leaders did accept John as a great prophet and were content to bask in his light for a while. This unmasks their duplicity. JB had acknowledged that Jesus' testimony was greater than his (3:27, 31–36).

Next, Jesus' miracles are brought forward as testimony. They prove his claims since they reveal His life-giving mission from the Father, and they have seen examples. Nevertheless the Jewish leaders deliberately refuse to accept the message of the miracles. They are interested in the spectacular element but not in the revelatory aspect. They refuse to learn from the Son.

Then there is the Father Himself. The people of God on Sinai had not seen the Face of God, nor had they heard His voice above the din of thunder and lightning (Deuteronomy 4:12, 15). Yet there God had given them the Law through Moses, and this Law testifies to Jesus. If the unnamed feast in this incident is Pentecost, then they were celebrating the giving of the Law on Sinai, which would make this discussion very appropriate. But the Law is no longer alive in their hearts, as the Word is alive in believers (Letter to Hebrews 4:12), so they cannot hear the internal testimony of the Father either (1 John 5:9–10). Believers carry the testimony of God alive in their own hearts where the Word is allowed to do its life-giving work in transforming them into images of the Son (Romans 8:29).

The fourth witness is the scriptures, which clearly come from God and therefore form part of the Father's witness. All the scriptures converge on Jesus, who is their fulfilment (1:49, 2:22, 5:39, 46, 12:16, 41, 19:28, 20:9). Yet with all this help the Jewish leaders refuse to come to Jesus for life, and by their influence they keep the people away also. They have the prophecies and the promises of God but refuse the fulfilment.

Causes of Unbelief (5:41–47)

Jesus went on a frontal attack exposing the real motive behind their unbelief, which was pride. They had not allowed the Love of God to enter their lives and soften their hearts. Hence when the Father sent His Beloved Son among them in a show of infinite love they refused to accept Him, although their history shows that they allowed themselves to be deceived by many false "messiahs". The refusal to give oneself to God is a choice of "self", that egocentric principle that keeps us in the "below" of the cosmos. In their egocentricity they glorified their great rabbis, and obviously those rabbis on the way up the scale deliberately sought this glory from others, thus forfeiting the only true "glory", that which comes from God. By contrast, it is the Father who glorifies Jesus, and Jesus only claims to be a reflection of this glory (1:14, 17:1).

Jesus used His trump card then as He attacked the Jewish leaders on their most sensitive point. They claimed to be followers of Moses (9:29), yet Moses had explicitly said that God would send them a prophet like himself, and they were to listen to him (Deuteronomy 18:15–18). Besides, the scriptures in general testify to Jesus. Jewish tradition claimed that Moses would intercede before God for the Jewish people, but Jesus claimed that Moses would condemn them instead, for refusing to accept what the scriptures had promised. If they refused to believe the lesser prophets how could they accept the Word of the Son? (Luke 16:29).

Chapter 6
Bread from Heaven

The fourth sign of the coming New Age is given at Passover, when all Israel celebrates the events which were central to their religious history, namely that God saved them from slavery through the prophet Moses. His great miracle ministry won their ancestors over to the Word of God. After the first Passover they followed Moses into the new life in the wilderness where he fed them with manna from heaven, and miraculous water from the rock, etc. In setting the miracle of the loaves in this context, it is obvious that John is presenting Jesus as the New Moses, or the Prophet-like-Moses whom the people were expecting. If he really *is* the Messiah, then He must perform a manna miracle to prove His claim.

Chapter six gives us many parallels between Jesus and Moses. The question Jesus put to Philip, "Where can we buy some bread for these people to eat?" resembles Numbers 11:13 where Moses asked God where he could get enough food for the nation. As the people grumbled against Moses and his food, so they will against Jesus (Numbers 11:1, 6:41–43). Both of them describe the manna as bread from heaven, but Jesus claims that Moses' miracle merely foreshadowed His (Numbers 11:7–9, 6:31). Other points of similarity show that both claim to give the people "flesh" to eat (Numbers 11:13, 6:51). And in Numbers 11:23 Moses wondered whether, if all the fish in the sea were gathered, it would suffice to feed them (6:9). Just as Moses crossed the sea, so too Jesus will cross the Sea of Galilee, but His walking on the water will reveal who He is to His disciples.

The Sign of the Bread (6:1–15)

It is obvious then that we are embarking on a sign that must be seen from "above" in order to get its full significance. As long as the people view it from "below" they misinterpret it, and only want a continuance of material bread which would solve nothing, and have no transforming effect on their lives.

Jesus came down to the Sea of Galilee (called Tiberias in later history). It was on the shores of this garden lake that He gave this sign. The hillside that Jesus climbed represents the Christian "Sinai", where the people meet God in Jesus, hear His Word and witness His signs. The Galilean crowds who follow Him there are just like those in Jerusalem, miracle-hungry, but not seeing beyond the sign to what it signified. The rejection of the Beloved Son is by all Israel then, not just its leaders. The beginnings shown here later develop to the point where the Beloved Son has to die.

Philip, who was from Bethsaida (1:44), was asked "from where" they should buy bread to feed these people. If he has been with Jesus from the beginning (as we have) he would reply "from above", from Your realm where the glory and Presence of God will be revealed in the action. But he replied "from below" and said that it would take two hundred days' wages to feed them. In other words it can't be done! The egocentric world cannot feed the world, since it has no love or power nor the creative Presence of God to supply what is necessary. It leaves the hungry to starve, the sick to die, and the sinner to perish.

The solution comes from the realm of Incarnate Love. No amount of money can buy bread from heaven – it has to come from the realm of "above". A little boy is willing to part with his five barley loaves and two fish, which was the food of the poor, and probably represented his food for that day. This gift of love formed a fitting base for the revelation of the Eucharistic gift by which Jesus will feed the starving multitudes. The simplicity of the child enabled him to come up to Jesus' level of Love with its limitless possibilities, where the intellectual approach of the adult prevented this. The disciples made it clear that they did not think the boy had the answer. "But what is that among so many?" they said, echoing Moses' inability to believe that God could accomplish such a feat.

Jesus ordered them to make the people sit down. John says that as many as five thousand men were present. The Jews never counted women or children, so if they were *also* present we have a vast multitude, and a great sign. In an obvious allusion to the Christian Eucharist in the early Church (John gives no actual account of the Eucharist at the Last Supper), Jesus took the loaves, gave thanks, and distributed them Himself to the waiting crowds – as He did at the Last Supper (Luke 22:19–20) – and did the same with the fish. When they had eaten as much as they wanted, for the miracle continued until the need was met, Jesus ordered the disciples to gather up the scraps left over, as happened at the Eucharistic celebration in the early Church (Didache 9:3–4).

They filled twelve large baskets from five barley loaves that had been given away in love, then blessed by the Lord and broken to feed the needy. The figure twelve symbolizes the foundation of the New Israel in the Twelve Apostles, who must learn the secret of feeding the world, as the little boy had done, for it was Jesus' intention to feed the starving multitudes of every generation. The gift of themselves given to the Lord, then blessed and broken, was all that was needed to let Divine Love loose in the cosmos. Then the world would experience the divine abundance it so badly needed. What a tragedy to prevent the New Order from taking over!

The people saw the sign from the material angle only, and said that Jesus must be the prophet they were expecting. How wonderful to have an endless supply of bread and not have to work! But Jewish nationalism had expectations that this prophet would be a political leader, and certain elements in Israel expected another davidic king to appear at Passovertime. Jesus fled from such an interpretation of His mission, and hid for safety, as a crowd this size would be dangerous when excited. How sad when the Lord has to flee from us because of what we will do to Him, due to the religious theories we concoct from our unseeing eyes. He will *have* to open the eyes of the blind if we are not to distort everything He says and does.

The Sign on the Lake (6:16–21)

Just as everything in Israel became a vehicle of revelation to the Chosen People, so too the Lake of Galilee was a symbol of life, with its two shores, one earthly and the other heavenly. The boat journeys speak of the spiritual journey of the people of God in the New Age, with the Apostles manning the boat. In all of the gospels we have boat scenes, and they make a fascinating study of the future mission of the Church. Usually the Apostles are experiencing difficulty, either it is a head wind against them or an outright storm. They are in danger of death themselves but also of the boat going down. They are represented as unable to catch fish even though they are professional fishermen – an indication of the difficult mission ahead, where it would be impossible to bring forth fruit except under the Lord's direction.

Jesus is often absent as in this scene, but sometimes He is asleep in the boat, apparently not caring about the trouble, yet he does come to the rescue in the end and they bring the boat safely to the other (heavenly) shore with its miraculous catch of fish, only to find Jesus waiting on the shore to meet them! (Chapter 21). All of this reflects the distress of the early first-century Church, which was battling with persecution and trying to cope with the physical absence of

Jesus, while firmly believing that He would come to them in the Parousia and bring the Bride home. That would be when the world would finally know who Jesus was, and who the Community of the beloved disciples was too.

That evening the disciples went down to the shore of the sea and got into a boat to make for Capernaum on the other side of the sea. It was getting dark by now and Jesus had still not joined them. The wind was strong and the sea was rough. The disciples had witnessed a great sign that day which they had not understood. The darkness outside merely reflected their continuing blindness and incomprehension. They went down to the lake and Jesus went up to the mountain to pray (Matthew 14:23). This represents the present state of the Church where the Community are on their journey and Jesus is at the right hand of the Father, ever living to make intercession for us (Letter to Hebrews 7:25). They are involved down "below" and He is involved up "above". They are having difficulty because they should have taken that day's revelation with them into the sea of life, but they did not. Jesus will have to join them and further reveal Himself, so that they take His "above" principles with them on their mission down "below" and then everything will work out.

They had rowed three or four miles when they saw Jesus walking on the water coming towards the boat. They were afraid but He said, "It's Me. Don't be afraid." They had completed most of their journey when they saw the impossible again, and were once more confronted with a whole new way of looking at reality. Jesus' power over the wind and the waves, revealed His I AM quality, which called them forth from the darkness of their unbelief to come to Him where He is on the level of "above", thus allowing God's creative power to operate in them. They accepted, and wanted to take Him into the boat. Literally, they now decided to "take him on board" with all that that meant for the transformation of their consciousness and lives. No wonder then that John says that they immediately reached the shore they were making for! Each one of us must take Jesus "on board" if our lives are to be transformed, and the so-called "impossible" become our normal life, as we allow the limitless possibilities of divine love to enter into every detail of our existence.

The Bread of Life (6:22–40)

We must view the following discourse in the light of the two preceding signs if we are to understand it. There we saw Jesus manifest Himself as the new Moses who gives us the new Manna, yet one greater than Moses because He is the "I AM". The Galilean crowds seek Jesus for the wrong reasons, because they have had enough bread to eat. Jesus will meet them, and help them to see beyond the bread they eat, to their saving Lord. They wonder how He could reach Capernaum without having a boat, but we the readers know how Jesus accomplished this feat.

Jesus asks the people to come up to His level and work for the food that will last, like the living water, unto eternal life. This food, which has this "above" quality, is the gift of the Son of Man Himself, who was given God's "seal", namely the fullness of the Spirit in His Baptism (which was not specifically mentioned by John). All earthly food is transient, like life itself. One must choose that which outlasts life, the food which has the transcendent quality that Jesus offers. Perishable food is for perishable life: Jesus' food is for eternal life.

The people now ask Jesus the key question: "*What are we to do if we are to carry out God's work*?" John has already told us the work of the Father – which was to send His Beloved Son into the unbelieving cosmos in order to save it (3:16). The work of the Son is to co-operate with the Father in the Salvation of all (4:34, 5:18, 17:4, 19:30). But what is the "work" of human beings? What must they do in this great plan? The "work" required of us is that we penetrate the mystery of the person of Jesus, internalize His teaching in our lives, and then put it into practice. This is to believe "in the one He has sent". It is not until they begin to open their ears to His teaching and their lives to His principles that they will understand what He can provide for time as well as eternity.

The crowds are nowhere near that openness of faith, and so they demand another sign, big enough for the sight of it to "*make us believe in you . . . Our fathers ate Manna in the desert*; *as scripture says*: *He gave them bread from heaven to eat*." Obviously the people were thinking of the many references in the rabbinic writings to a Manna miracle in the New Age to come. Did they think that the multiplication of the loaves should continue, as the Manna had done for forty years? If this is the same crowd that had witnessed the miracle yesterday they are certainly not satisfied with a sign that is spiritual. They want something material in their hands, now, that would force faith upon them. The unsatisfactory nature of this position needs no explanation.

In the discussion which follows Jesus answers them point by point, as was done in the Jewish homily at that time. First, He points out that it was the Father, not Moses, who provided the Manna in the desert (Exodus 16:4,15; Psalm 78:24; Wisdom 16:20–21). The same Father has now sent His Beloved Son Jesus to give life to the world. A flashback to His signs will remind us of His life-giving powers, as will a preview of the chapters ahead. Like the woman of Samaria, the crowds request Jesus to provide this food from heaven, and they want it "always", even though they do not grasp its nature. Yet this is precisely why Jesus came. The great "I AM" is food for His people, food to satisfy the deepest longings of the human heart (see Deuteronomy 8:2–3; Wisdom 16:26).

"*I am the bread of life. No one who comes to Me will ever hunger; no one who believes in Me will ever thirst.*" Jesus *is*

God's bread sent down from heaven, and He invites everyone to come to His table. John appears to present Jesus in this discourse both as the bread of God's Word and as the Eucharistic bread of life. Thus there is a double strain running throughout. In the Old Testament God's Word was often referred to as "food" (Proverbs 9:4–6; Sirach 15:3; Wisdom 16:26: Isaiah 55:11), but Jesus surpasses all the food of the Old Testament, since He IS the Father's Word to them. His words do not just give information about God, they contain the mystery of God and the Presence of God. When one listens humbly and openly one experiences that Presence and Life in oneself.

Yet these Galilean people are no better than the Jerusalem crowds, for they too do not believe. Jesus informs them that those who "come to Him" are really the Father's gift to Him (17:6), and He will reject no one, because He is here to do the Father's will. Anyone who will penetrate the mystery of Jesus and believe in Him, will not only receive the gift of life now but will also be raised up on the last day. There is a gift for now and then.

Decision Time (6:41–71)

Meanwhile the Jews were complaining to each other about Him, because He had said, "I am the bread that has come down from heaven". They were saying, "Surely this is Jesus son of Joseph, whose father and mother we know. How can He now say, 'I have come down from heaven'?" As we have seen already on this journey, Jesus' light shows up the secret thoughts of many hearts, and discriminates between those who choose God's way and those who do not. Just so here. The Jewish leaders react to Jesus' words by complaining that He not only did not come down from heaven, but they knew where He really did come from (geographically), and they also knew His parents. Besides, he was only a carpenter Himself, so His claims are spurious. Their misunderstanding regarding His origins enables Jesus to explain, but He answers the question on His own level, thus trying to bring them "up" to a position of faith.

The murmuring of the Jews indicates a refusal to believe, and if they would open their hearts to God's action they would soon realize that they are living in the age prophesied by Isaiah, when *they would all be taught by God* (Isaiah 54:13). If they were open to God's word in the Old Testament, and allowed the Father to move their hearts by His revelation as He said He would (Jeremiah 33:31–33), they would realize that it was embodied in Jesus just now for them. He is the only one who has seen the Father, and can guarantee eternal life. Their ancestors who enjoyed Moses' manna are all dead, for it was only earthly food, though provided in a miraculous way, but the bread of Jesus is eternal. Those who eat it will not die. This bread is not only given miraculously, but it is of a different quality to the manna. It is from "above" while the manna was from "below". The food that Jesus gives is His own flesh, His own person, through which He imparts life to all who partake of it.

"*In all truth I tell you, if you do not eat the flesh of the Son of man and drink His blood, you have no life in you. Anyone who does eat My flesh and drink My blood has eternal life.*" Naturally the unbelieving Jews accuse Jesus of cannibalism, because eating flesh and blood, materially speaking, was incomprehensible to them, as well as unlawful (Leviticus 17:11–14). An understanding of the mystery would require post-resurrection knowledge. Jesus is speaking from the "above" level of the limitless possibilities of divine love, whereby He will, through the Eucharistic miracle, feed His beloved disciples on, not just His word, but Himself, His own person.

A refusal to accept this gift is a refusal to accept the new life, because Jesus' Body and Blood are *real* food and drink, which brings about an intimate union with Him. In fact this gift enables the disciples to *draw life* from Jesus just as He draws life from the Father. This bread, therefore, cannot be compared to the manna which was only a pale shadow of it. In Jesus' Word they can listen to and hear Jesus, but in the Eucharistic Bread they *have* Him present to them. He has given Himself to us as Word and bread.

Jesus taught this in the synagogue at Capernaum, but His audience found it intolerable. The manna was for the past, the messianic banquet for the future, and wisdom's banquet was for the chosen few. What was this? – cannibalism or the Wisdom of Divine Love? Was it so far beneath them or so far above them? Whichever it was, they were not going to risk it, so they walked away from one of the greatest manifestations of God's Love conceivable.

Jesus wonders how, if they are so unable to accept this sign of God's Love for them, they will react when the final proof that Jesus came down from heaven is given by His ascension to heaven again? His lifting up on the cross will not be the end, but only a prelude to His lifting up in glory. "*It is the spirit that gives life, the flesh has nothing to offer. The words I have spoken to you are spirit and life.*" They *must* come to realize that it is only on the level of "spirit" or "above" that these gifts can be given by Jesus, or accepted by His disciples. The flesh level of "below" has nothing to offer, nor any power to comprehend. Jesus' words are both spirit-filled and life-giving, and can therefore bring about that which they promise.

The mystery of the human response continues, with Jesus losing some of His disciples in the general walk-out that followed. He reminded those who stayed that they needed help from "above" to see. Jesus then challenged His "twelve" about their commitment to him. *Then Jesus said to the Twelve, "What about you, do you want to go away too?"* He would constrain no one to stay with Him. Simon Peter rose to the occasion and spoke on behalf of them all, that there was no one else they could go to. "Jesus", he said, was the "Holy One of God", therefore the Messiah, in unique relationship to God. This is a good counterbalance to the unconverted bread-seekers at Capernaum, but Jesus is never over-impressed by human nature, knowing its fickleness.

There are two movements going on now. One is decision time, both for those who will go with Peter all the way, and for those who walk away. The treachery of those who reject Jesus was already seen in their plot to kill Him at the pool of Bethesda (5:16–18). It will culminate in the action of Judas, which, for all its secrecy, will not surprise Jesus. Obviously some in John's church were tempted to look back to Moses, but it was decision time for them, and they are challenged to go all the way with Peter instead. The Church has made its decision that Jesus *alone* had the message of eternal life. Those individuals who are still undecided are asked to follow Peter, and warned of what happened to those who rejected Jesus initially.

Chapter 7

Whence Comes the Son of Man?

As we move deeper into the gospel John prepares us for the coming events of Jesus' death and what that means for us. The mood of tension increases and will become sustained. Yet Jesus remains calm and in control, constantly revealing Himself and faithful to His Father's mission. By now, after five signs – the discourses with Nicodemus, the Samaritan woman, the Galilean crowds, and the presentation of witnesses to the Jerusalem authorities – we the readers have no doubt who Jesus is, or whence He came. We have grown accustomed to His actions done in tandem with the Father, and so *we know* that His origins go far beyond His geographical home in Nazareth.

We remember too that He was introduced in the Prologue as the Light of the World, light which is opposed by the darkness of sin and unbelief. We have witnessed people take one of the two options open to them, namely to accept or reject the light, and we have seen that those who reject become hostile and want to put the light out. The struggle reaches greater intensity now as the people debate whether Jesus offers *too little*, meaning that their political ambitions will not be fulfilled in Him, or *too much*, since He wants to change everything – new wine, new life, new Temple, living water, bread from heaven, eternal life, as if He himself were the source of all these blessings.

John wants us to see that the death Jesus suffered was no accident. It was deliberately orchestrated by those who chose the darkness over the light. As we proceed it will seem that the darkness wins unless our eyes have been opened to what is happening on the supernatural level, where God is at work. We already know that it is impossible for the darkness to overcome the light (1:5), but when Jesus surrenders into the hands of His enemies we will need to remember this. The powers of darkness will think they have the upper hand, but the reality is that Jesus and the Father are accomplishing the salvation of the world through these same events, unnoticed by the enemy.

In the following chapters the "darkness" will show itself in the sheer refusal to "see", in stubborn unwillingness to recognize any good in Jesus or any truth in His claims. As far as His enemies are concerned he is earth-born, demon-possessed and blasphemous, a man who dares to teach publicly without even a proper education! They deliberately misunderstand him and make wild accusations, causing confusion among the people who see Jesus as a prophet. But is theirs a correct judgement on Jesus? We know Him to be the Beloved Son of the Father who has rested on the Father's bosom for all eternity. In all that follows we must remain on Jesus' level of seeing from "above" if we are truly to discern who He is.

Tabernacles (7:1–13)

The drama is set against the Feast of Tabernacles, the autumnal harvest feast, which lasted eight days. It was one of the three great pilgrimage feasts which the people were expected to celebrate in Jerusalem. It was also called the feast of Booths or Tents. The people erected huts to live in for the duration of the feast, to commemorate the years of wandering in the wilderness (Leviticus 23:39; Deuteronomy 16:13). In Jesus' time the celebrations combined both water rites and a feast of lights. It is the deeper meaning of this feast that provides Jesus (and John) with the opportunity to reveal further who Jesus really is.

It is harvest time, and the people give thanks to God for His blessings, but they do not discern that the true Harvest of God's Kingdom has arrived in Jesus, that He is the real reason why anyone should give thanks to God! During the feast water was carried in procession from the Pool of Siloam, and poured over the altar, both in thanksgiving and in request for rain to provide the future harvests. At night the Temple was illuminated with torches so that it was bathed in light for the duration of the feast. It was in thanksgiving to God for being their "Light" and their source of "Life" (water).

It was also the time of thanksgiving for the renewal of the Covenant when the synagogue readings referred to the Exodus and the water miracles granted to their ancestors (Exodus 17:1–7; Psalm 78:15–16). During the feast the expectancy of the Messiah ran high. Indeed, even in later centuries the rabbis held that this feast contained within it the promise of the Messiah. He would fulfil Ezekiel's vision (chapter 47) of abundant water flowing from the Temple. What better occasion could Jesus have than to present Himself as the one who gives the abundant living waters? As the Light of the World? As the One sent by God when even the Pool of Siloam bore His name, "the One Sent"? As the new Temple from which the living waters flow?

John begins by reminding us that it was dangerous for Jesus to go to Judaea (5:18), so He waited until the Feast of Tabernacles, some months after Pentecost. His relatives in Galilee did not understand him (7:5). They were still in the darkness of worldly thinking, and urged Jesus to reveal Himself to the world, without realizing that on the spiritual level of "above", that is precisely why He came. They just wanted Him to do more spectacular miracles to "make" people accept Him as Messiah, which would have advantages for them as His family. But we have already seen that miracles don't produce faith, so Jesus rejected this motive for going to Jerusalem. Since they are still in the darkness of unbelief they can go to Jerusalem any time. The unbelieving world (cosmos) has no reason to hate them. On the other hand, Jesus is preparing for a definite visit to Jerusalem which will happen in God's time, His Hour, a visit that will bring everything to a head, when He will ascend not only to Jerusalem, but to the cross, and then into the Father's presence; but that is not for now.

The temptations of Jesus which are given dramatically in Matthew and Luke (chapter 4) are illustrated here. The Synoptic gospels speak of three temptations. John shows two of them in chapter six and the third one here. In 6:15 the people wanted to make Jesus king: in Matthew 4:8 Satan offered him the kingdoms of the world. The people ask for miraculous bread in 6:34, while Satan asked Jesus to turn stones into bread in Matthew 4:3. Here the brothers ask Him to show His power in Jerusalem, while Satan asked Him to display His power by jumping from the parapet of the Temple in Matthew 4:5. John seems to imply that the temptations came to Jesus in the normal course of His life, just as it happens for us. Like us, He had to see through each suggestion made to Him and discern what was really being asked. As we have seen, He fled from any insinuation that would deflect Him from His Father's will.

Later Jesus went up to Jersualem quietly and found great discussion going on regarding Him. Everyone was looking out for Him, but it was all in secret, for even the people were afraid of the hostility of the leaders to Jesus.

Mistaken Identity (7:14–36)

As the trial of Jesus continues to take place in public, in the Temple of God, we have a double stage to deal with. In the foreground Jesus tries to teach and convince the crowds, while in the background the Jewish leaders plot His death. For this reason John will not give us a trial of Jesus before the Sanhedrin during the passion as we see the drama played out here to its conclusion. There John will merely convene the Sanhedrin to ratify the judgement passed on Him here. The "works" of light and darkness go on side by side, and one needs eyes that "see", for the interpretation of events depends on whether we are the frontstage or backstage participators.

When the festival was half-over Jesus presented Himself in the Temple to teach, but He had never studied under the rabbis. In fact, because He was uneducated He had no right to teach. In those days it was expected that a teacher would be able to respond to problems by giving the answers of the famous rabbis who had gone before him, but Jesus never quoted anybody. His teaching came, so it seemed, from Himself, and since He was uneducated how COULD He pronounce on the Law of Moses? *Jesus answered them*: "*My teaching is not from myself*: *it comes from the one who sent me . . .* " Jesus' answer is what we expect now, that He has been to the greatest of all schools, and His Teacher is none other than the Father. He Himself is the "one sent" from the Father, and therefore the right one to interpret Him, and His view of God's Law.

Going on the attack, Jesus accused the leaders of not keeping the very Law they boasted about. It was their duty to discern a true from a false prophet, so their intention to kill Jesus broke God's commandment, since He is not only "a" true prophet, but their Messiah. Some of the crowd, perhaps many of the pilgrims, were unaware of the plot to kill Jesus, but Jesus knew that the desire of the leaders to do away with Him was on account of His healing on the Sabbath. John gives only one example of this in chapter five, but the synoptics show that Jesus consistently broke the Sabbath. He must explain why, for this was a serious crime in their eyes.

The Sabbath was the sacred day of rest, yet the rabbis allowed circumcision to take place on that day. They spoke of circumcision as "the healing of a member", both in the sense of the physical body and of that person's entrance into the People of God. Jesus' reply was that the whole purpose of the Sabbath in God's eyes is the healing of the whole person in salvation, a thing He demonstrated in His healing of the cripple. He appealed to them again to see things from God's point of view. We must ask whether it is more important to celebrate the Sabbath or experience it? To celebrate a ritual or experience its inner meaning? Jesus demonstrated the deepest meaning of the Sabbath in His healing ministry.

Now the trial shifts on to the question of Jesus' origins. The normal Jerusalem crowds are aware of the plot to kill Jesus, and they wonder whether the authorities have made up their minds as to whether He is the Christ. The problem was that the people knew the Messiah would be born in Bethlehem, and many believed that he would remain hidden until he appeared in public. But Jesus who is standing before them IS their hidden Messiah, whose real origins are unknown to them, since He has come from heaven. But they are thinking on the level of "below", and as far as they are concerned He is only from Nazareth. They were told not to judge by appearances (verse 24), yet that is precisely what they do now. In FACT they do not know where Jesus comes from, nor do they realize His intimate relationship with the Father. This claim results in the first attempt to arrest Him, but they have no power to do so (though they are unaware of this) until His Hour comes.

The futile attempt at arresting Jesus brings up the subject of His impending departure. The crowds are divided about Him. As usual some believe but others do not. Jesus warns them that they have only a short time now to make up their minds, as He will soon return to the Father, and if they stay on the level of unbelief they will have no way of comprehending what has taken place in their midst, either in the incarnation of the Son of God or in His "lifting up". And they will be unable to follow Him into the new life, because unbelief keeps them in the dark which cannot comprehend the light. The leaders misunderstand, thinking that Jesus intends to go abroad among the Jews of the Dispersion to teach the Gentiles. Unconsciously they have stumbled on a great truth, for after the resurrection Christianity will, indeed, "go abroad" to the Gentiles, who will listen eagerly to its message and receive the new life that Jesus offered, while the Jewish nation will have, as a whole, missed all that Jesus came for. So then, if they look for Him materially or spiritually He will no longer be found, because they have missed their chance. It is decision time for them, now, as a nation. The very Church that John is writing for is "away" among the diaspora, and most of his converts were the despised Gentiles who had eagerly taken the new life of Jesus.

Water from the Rock (7:37–52)

The moment of highest drama at this festival has come, when the ancient prophecies were alive in the hearts of the people, and their expectations keen. If one reads the prophet Zechariah, chapters 9–14, one will see the backdrop from which Jesus cried out to the nation of Israel that He, and He alone, was the fulfilment of all that had been promised to them. Zechariah told the people that their Messianic king would come to Jerusalem (9:9), that he would open up a fountain for the house of David (13:1), and that living waters would flow from Jerusalem (14:8). Then they would keep this Feast of Tabernacles properly (14:16), Jerusalem would be cleansed (13:1), and there would be no more traders in the Temple (14:21).

Jesus stood and cried out: "*Let anyone who is thirsty come to Me*! *Let anyone who believes in Me come and drink*! *As scripture says*, '*from his heart shall flow streams of living water*'." *He was speaking of the Spirit which those who believed in Him were to receive* . . . Now, on the last and greatest day of the festival, as the solemn procession returned from Siloam and approached the altar of God, Jesus took His stand (and He only a rustic teacher from Galilee!), and cried out from the depths of His being (indeed from the depths of God) so loudly, that all Israel heard that their Messiah HAD come to the Temple, that their prayers for water HAD been heard by God, but in a way that surpassed all expectation (Ephesians 3:21). Jesus proclaimed himself the *ROCK* which would be struck (19:34) to provide the living water for ANYONE who thirsted for God (hence He is the Saviour of all the world, as the Samaritans discovered). This will release the Fountain of Life which will flow from the right side of the New Temple (Ezekiel 47) which is His Body (2:21). Their ancestors had miraculous water given them in torrents when Moses struck the rock (Psalm 78:15–20). Now Jesus claimed that just as the manna in the desert merely foreshadowed HIS bread, so too, the rock in the desert prepared them for this moment of wonder (Revelation 7:17, 22:1). John explains that this gift will be given in Jesus' Hour, when He will pour out the gift of the Holy Spirit upon the community of the beloved disciples.

Naturally one would expect strong reaction to this, especially since we know that the leaders are still on the side of darkness and unbelief. From "below" Jesus' words and actions will appear different from what they really are. A heated debate ensued, when one might have expected thanksgiving! To some He was the prophet-like-Moses, but to others He had the wrong credentials, as the subject of His origins has not been solved. The people are not aware that Jesus HAS, in fact, been born in Bethlehem, the town of David; they think He was born in Nazareth.

The utter frustration of the leaders is illustrated by the guards who were sent to arrest Jesus, but who returned without having made the arrest. After listening to His words, the police gave testimony to Him instead! "*No one has ever spoken like this man*", they said. The leaders resorted to scorn and sarcasm, showing that they despised the ordinary people who were not well versed in the Law, and therefore would break the Law many times unknowingly. The fact that THEY were impressed by Jesus meant nothing. Those who studied the Law, like the Sanhedrin, did not believe in Him. But to their surprise and chagrin Nicodemus stood up for Jesus' right to a proper hearing before judgement would be passed on Him. The Law they claimed to obey demanded this! (Deuteronomy 1:16, 17:4). Like Nathanael before them, they will not accept a prophet coming from Nazareth. But if they opened their hearts to Jesus as Nathanael had done, they too would see great things that would make them wonder, and give praise to God, instead of being the agents for His destruction.

Chapter 8
Unwelcome Light

The Merciful Judge (8:1–11)

Stuck right in the middle of the great controversy is a scene of delicate beauty, which probably was not part of the original gospel, but an insertion from a later date. It depicts Jesus in the role of merciful judge, illustrating some of the teaching in this chapter. For example in 8:16 Jesus says that He judges no one, but if He is forced to judge He will give true justice. In 8:46 He challenges His opponents to try to convict Him of sin if they can. Here in this scene Jesus' enemies both force Him to judge a woman and try to use her to catch Him in some error. They succeed only in showing us, the readers, how unworthy they are as witnesses and accusers in the trial of the Beloved Son. Throughout Jesus remains serene and majestic, as He will in His passion and execution later. John contrasts the gentle mercy of Jesus with the cynical unfeeling zeal for the letter of the Law in the men who bring the case for judgement.

The prophet Daniel has a similar story in the case of Susanna, who was falsely accused of adultery by two men. The Law demanded death by stoning for such a crime (Leviticus 20:10; Deuteronomy 22:21; Daniel 13). Susanna prayed to God for justice to be done, and the Lord touched Daniel to come to her aid by exposing her accusers. Since she was innocent she could appeal for justice, but to whom shall the sinner go, since she is guilty? If we parallel these two stories we notice that "I AM" has the answer for both the guilty AND the innocent. The innocent can appeal to justice, and the guilty ask for mercy and forgiveness. St Augustine's comment on this scene deserves mention: on that day great misery met great mercy – *Misera* met *Misericordia*.

John places this incident during the Feast of Tabernacles when Jesus was staying out on the Mount of Olives, which enabled Him to go to the Temple very early each morning to teach. As the people gathered around Him they were interrupted by the leaders, who brought a woman caught in the very act of committing adultery. This implies that a trap had been set for her, probably by her jealous husband and the witnesses who had conspired with him to catch her in her sin, instead of trying to win back her love by forgiveness (see Hosea 2:14–17, 3:1). Their unkindness will be shown up in Jesus' delicate handling of her. Again the light will show up the darkness and illuminate what is really there.

The problem is that they had not only set a trap for the woman but were using her to set a trap for Jesus! In the absence of Love they make both Jesus AND the woman victims of their unfounded zeal for a Law whose spirit they do not grasp. The fact that they take the case to Jesus for judgement illustrates that He had gained a reputation as a prophet, who will pronounce God's will. If Jesus decides in favour of the Mosaic law, then He will fall foul of the Romans, who had removed the power to impose and carry out the death penalty from the Sanhedrin. He will also fail in mercy and kindness to the sinner, and we know from the Synoptic gospels that Jesus had quite a reputation as a friend of sinners (Luke 7:34). If He decides against the Law, then He will have to face the Sanhedrin (Mark 12:13–17 for a parallel case).

But Jesus bent down and started writing on the ground with His finger. This strange gesture has been variously interpreted, but it seems to be a prophetic action that the men understood. Some think that Jesus wrote the words of Jeremiah 17:13: "O Lord, the hope of Israel, all who forsake you will be put to shame. Those who turn away from you will be written in the dust because they have forsaken the Lord, the fountain of living water" (NIV). This would fit John's general theme in these chapters.

Jesus then pronounced His impartial judgement. If they are to initiate the stoning according to Deuteronomy 17:7 they must be free of the sin themselves. They must be KEEPERS of the Law not just executors of it! In any case the sinner has no right to judge another (Matthew 7:1), for how can darkness discriminate correctly? Only the light can do that, as Jesus illuminates the consciences of these men, who slip away as quietly as they can. I wonder if the crowd (whom we have probably forgotten!) grasped the real meaning of the law as properly administered? Did they recognize the new Solomon?

At last there remained only the sinner and the saviour. Jesus addressed her with the same honour that He gave to all women in this gospel. "*Woman*", *He said*, "*where are they? Has no one condemned you?*" "*No one, sir*", *she replied*. "*Neither do I condemn you*", *said Jesus*. "*Go away, and from THIS MOMENT sin no more.*" Jesus seems almost surprised that He has managed to save her. He wants to be sure that all the men are gone, before He lifts her on to His plane, where New Life awaits her. Those on the level of darkness chose death for her, but Love offered her life, so we can see the difference between what the unbelieving cosmos and the Beloved Son offer. Death or life? The lostness of "below" or the limitless possibilities of "above"? The old order would rid itself of such a woman as a blight on the land (Deuteronomy 22:21), but Jesus came to re-create heaven in the human heart, to take away the devastation of sin and replace it with eternal life.

The woman is given a second chance, but like all the others who meet Jesus, she must choose the new way. Her old sin-life must go. Jesus does not condone her sin, which was the way of darkness and destruction. He forgives it, thereby releasing her from its chains, and making it possible for her to choose real life. From *that moment* all the possibilities of the life from "above" are available to one who was considered a "write-off". That is a marvellous demonstration of the fact that the Lord's ways are as different from ours as the heavens are from the earth (Isaiah 55:9). The healing of the physical cripple was only a step towards the reality demonstrated here, which reveals Jesus as the Redeemer.

Light and Darkness in Conflict (8:12–30)

During the Feast of Tabernacles there was a celebration of God as the Light of the World. In the Court of the Women, where Jesus now proclaims Himself the Light of the World, they lit four huge golden candlesticks and four large basins in which they floated wicks. The light from these was said to have illuminated the whole of Jerusalem at night, and communicated a wonderful glowing sense of God's Presence among the people. In this way they commemorated the fact that God IS Light (Psalm 27:1; Baruch 5:9), and the author of Light (Genesis 1:3–5; Psalm 36:9; etc), also that God had manifested Himself to their ancestors in the desert by a Pillar of Light (Exodus 13:21–22). Zechariah had foretold that the Messiah would usher in a New Age of perpetual light (Zechariah 14:6–7), and on top of this they knew that the Torah, the Word of God, gave "light" or enlightenment to those who lived it. In fact Wisdom 18:3–4 speaks of the Pillar of Light as given to those through whom "*the incorruptible light of the Law was to be given to the world*".

It is against this background that Jesus announced that both God's Word and God's Light are available in and through Him for everyone. In Him they have God's total light, His fullest revelation, the New Torah, to guide them into all truth. In accepting Jesus they lose nothing, for in

Him they ALSO have the Father on their side. Not only has Jesus offered life-giving water, and life-giving bread, but now He offers life-giving Light, which He will demonstrate in healing the blind man in the next chapter.

"*I am the light of the world; anyone who follows Me will not be walking in the dark but will have the light of life.*" The God of Moses, the great "I AM", had been present in the Pillar of Light, as they knew He was invisibly present in the Temple. How shocking then for them to hear an itinerant preacher from Galilee claim that He was that manifestation of the Father's Presence! The Light had come to the Temple, in Person, fulfilling yet surpassing all their expectations of the Messiah. They knew that their ancestors would have lost their way in the desert but for that Pillar of Light. Just so Jesus now informs them that they will lose their way spiritually if they do not follow Him who is the Pillar of Light among them. He alone knows the way to the Father, as we shall see in 14:6. God's Light shines forth in Him as the incarnate revealer, dispelling the darkness of unbelief and enlightening sinners regarding the true meaning of life.

The reaction is understandably vicious. Because His opponents are from "below" they do not grasp that Jesus is not alone and testifying on His own behalf, something not admissible in a trial (Deuteronomy 17:6, 19:15; Numbers 35:30). Lost in the darkness of unbelief they do not realize either "whence" He came or whither He is going, since only those who have received the new life know that Jesus came from the Father in heaven, and will return to Him after he has been "lifted up". All His actions are done in tandem with the Father, who is His real witness. Jesus' very presence among them provokes judgement in the sense that the light discriminates between believers and unbelievers, yet Jesus did not come in the Incarnation to be the apocalyptic judge who would condemn the wicked at the end of time. Nevertheless, His light makes people judge themselves here and now, as they opt for or against what He offers.

Since they have refused to recognize the Father in Jesus they show that they lack the intimate knowledge of God that they claimed to have under the Old Covenant. Such experiential knowledge of God would have enabled them to recognize "The Presence" in Jesus. In their blindness they want to extinguish the Light, but it is imperishable, unlike their own. Jesus urgently warns them that THIS is the DAY OF SALVATION for them, and if they finally refuse the light, then there is no other, and they will be left outside of God's great plan of redemption. Left to their egotism, blindness and unbelief, left in the cosmos with no answers to life's questions, left in their sin of unbelief, which is the basis of all other sins, because it is a refusal of life and growth.

Jesus is already on the way to the Father, and they cannot join Him for they are still "from below" and uncomprehending. All Jesus' words and actions find their origin and meaning from "above", and as long as the gulf exists between them they will have to go to their graves never knowing that the Messiah had come, bringing with Him all the blessings of the New Age. No matter how terrible it sounds, they must allow Him to confront them with the awesome reality that God is among us, that they are speaking to the same mystery that confronted Moses in the burning bush (Exodus 3). Jesus and the Father are One. They have only a short time now to make up their minds. After that it will be too late. A unique opportunity has been given to them which will not be repeated.

Blindness and unbelief provoke the question "*Who are you*?" which amazes anyone on the level of "above". From the beginning of the ministry Jesus has been proclaimed the Beloved Son. But the unbelievers will recognize Him only when it is too late. The mystery of His "lifting up" on the cross and in glory will fully reveal Him, but unfortunately this will be brought about by those who do not believe, and so they draw a terrible judgement on their heads for having murdered the One who was sent from the Father. Only then will they know that God has been in their midst wooing them with loving-kindness which they rejected. Then too they will realize that the Son worked in tandem with the Father, in total surrender of love, teaching only what He Himself was taught by God. They will see what the prophets had longed to see, namely a Son of God acting only to please the Father who was WITH HIM in such a unique way.

My Father and Your Father (8:31–59)

We reach the essence of the conflict now in the question of fatherhood. As usual we will hear the discussion on two levels: the Jews are interested in their privileged position as children of Abraham, which was no small honour, unless it is contrasted with the extraordinary honour of having God for your Father. No matter how great Abraham is he still comes from the realm of "below", as will be seen in the claims on a political and national level. The privileges and "home" of those who walk in the spirit are on the Father's level. On earth, being sons of Abraham really matters, but in heaven it is the Sons of God who hold sway. The searing light of the Son strikes very deep now, indeed at the core of their self-understanding as the people of God, and they resent it very much.

Three fathers are discussed: God, the heavenly Father, who is the giver of all life, truth, freedom and light; Abraham, who gave them national descent as the Chosen People; and Satan, the father of lies, deception and murder, the ruler of the sphere of darkness and unbelief. One can have the two fathers Abraham and God at the same time, but it is inconceivable to have all three. Jesus argues that from their fruits, from their actions, one can decipher the source or "father" one comes from (Matthew 7:20). This argument presumes fathers and sons are alike, just as Jesus and the Father are one in thought and action.

The background of this discussion is the fact that Abraham and his descendants were to be a blessing to the whole world (Genesis 22:17–18; Psalm 105:6). The sense of responsibility following this had been lost over the centuries, leaving only a claim to automatic divine protection, and privilege (Luke 16:24). The Synoptics deal with this problem also, saying that God could raise up children to Abraham from the stones (Matthew 3:7–10), while warning the Jews that other people would find their way into the Kingdom before them (Matthew 18:11–12). This reflects the sharp debates between the Jews and the Christians in the early Church, about whether Jesus was *sufficient*, whether He had ALL the light and life, in other words whether He was the ONLY Name by which we could be saved (Acts 4:12). We have been prepared for this by John in the Prologue, when he told us that in Moses (a symbol of the Synagogue) one receives ONLY the Law, but in Jesus one enters into the limitless possibilities of God's Life and Love (1:17).

True disciples of Jesus not only receive His word but abide in it. There they find all that is needed to set them free in the truest sense of that word, namely inwardly, where one can live a fully human life, yet on the level of the "divine" because its source is supernatural. Implicit here is that Jesus' word transcends the Law, and we find Paul passionately pleading with the early Christians to realize this (Galatians 5:1; Romans 7, 8:2). Jesus wants to set them free from the Law, but also from sin, which is the greatest slavery since it chains the inner man. The Law could only point out the wrong-doing, but not set anyone free from it. Only the Beloved Son had that right and privilege.

Typical of John, the Jews misunderstand Jesus, thinking He was speaking on the natural level. In their national pride they claim that they have never been slaves of anyone, even though they had been conquered successively by Assyria, Babylonia, Greece and Rome. But perhaps they mean that they were never inwardly enslaved by them, as their nation rose from death so often? Jesus keeps to His own level and declares that anyone who commits sin is a slave. And following the custom of the day he reminds them that the slaves' place in the house is not secure, therefore their national claim to a place in the Kingdom of God without producing the "works" of Abraham is spurious. Abraham had believed in God and obeyed His word. He received the messengers God sent to him (Genesis 12:4, 17–18), but his descendants have not received Jesus, nor have they believed His Word. Because of this they will destroy God's messenger, One who has been at the Father's side, One who has told them the truth as He learnt it from God Himself. Since that is so, they prove that Satan is their "father" since he is the power behind unbelief and darkness and the architect of Jesus' death.

It is not descent from Abraham according to the flesh that worries Jesus. He challenges their status as God's People. The Old Testament used the image of marriage to explain the relationship between God and His people, so infidelity to the Lord when they strayed after other gods was referred to as "fornication" or "adultery" (Hosea 2:4). If they as God's People allow God's arch-enemy, Satan, to keep them in the darkness of unbelief then they HAVE strayed, but as we have seen at the beginning of this chapter, Jesus is quite willing to forgive the sin and offer the sinner new life as of *this moment.*

"*We were not born illegitimate, the only father we have is God.*" This powerful retort carries not only a denial of infidelity to God, but an insinuation that there was something strange about Jesus' birth. They know that Israel is God's first-born son among the nations (Exodus 4:22), and God became their Father on Sinai (Deuteronomy 32:6).

All the prophets taught them the same: Isaiah told them that even "if Abraham will not own us . . . you, Lord, are our Father". On the principle that the son should be LIKE the father, Jesus completely disowns them as sons of God. His argument is that they would recognize the Beloved Son if they too were sons, for his origin is IN GOD.

Their hostility to His word shows that they have another more sinister father, the devil, who instigated the first murder, just as he is plotting the demise of the Beloved Son. In seeking to bring about the death of Jesus, the Jews are doing the devil's work for him. Deceit, not truth, is his "thing", and he has deceived them as to the reality of who Jesus is. There is no truth in him as he is opposed to it, whereas truth and holiness reside in Jesus, and they tried in vain to find sin or falsehood in Him.

Jesus challenged the Jews on who they really were. They in turn challenge who He really is, accusing Him of being a Samaritan AND possessed, thus implying that His signs were merely magical works whose origins were in the powers of evil. Thus they accuse Light of being Darkness, which is the unforgivable sin (Mark 3:22–30). The Samaritans were despised by the Jews as lovers of magic, so being a Samaritan AND possessed are almost the same thing, and both carry an accusation of uncleanness (Acts 8). Gently, Jesus replies that He honours the Father, and leaves it to the Father, the Person THEY call GOD, to honour Him. But anyone, and that includes Jesus' opponents, who receives Jesus' word will never see death because in the here and now of time, they will have already passed over from the realm of the unbelieving world to the Kingdom of God, where they participate in the New Life of God, which is indestructible like Himself.

This brings us to the highest point in the self-revelation of Jesus. His stunned audience realize that He is claiming to be greater than Abraham, who has been dead for about eighteen hundred years. Abraham had rejoiced to see the day of the Lord coming, which he saw in the birth of his son Isaac, who foreshadowed the long-awaited Messiah. The moment has come for Jesus solemnly to declare: "*In all truth I tell you, before Abraham ever was*, Ego Eimi." Far beyond the greatness of their ancient ancestor is the timeless eternity of the Beloved Son who pre-existed Abraham and rested on the Father's bosom from all eternity. Abraham's God is addressing them in Jesus!

Only Jesus and the Father ever said: *Ego Eimi*. No one else would dare appropriate the sacred name of God. No prophet, priest or king ever made such a statement, and standing before this mystery they had no choice but to fall at His feet or stone Him, depending what level they operate on. Sadly they pick up stones to stone Him, who is their greatest treasure – the glory of Israel. Darkness could not accept the unmerited forgiving loving-kindness of God our Saviour. All they can think of is blasphemy and the carrying out of the letter of the law. And Jesus must hide Himself again from a people who had cried out to God for a Messiah for two thousand years! There are none so blind as those who refuse to see.

Chapter 9

Light to the Blind / Blind to the Light

Breaking his usual pattern, John gives us the sixth sign after the discourse on light, rather than before it. Also, Jesus points out the meaning of the sign before it is given. This is a double sign, one half of which shows a man journeying from darkness to light, both physically and spiritually. It is also a tale of how those who thought they saw, the Pharisees, were plunging into deepening darkness because of their refusal of the light.

Jesus is the Light of the World (8:12, 9:5; see also Isaiah 49:6), the One who reveals *Ego Eimi* to the world in human form, the One who frees people from their darkness to enter into a new grace-relationship with the Father. Jesus demonstrates this in opening the man's eyes, for we discover that something even more beautiful happens to his inner person as he is enlightened regarding the mystery of Jesus, believes and worships Him. The story will demonstrate yet again that people have the option to accept or reject the light, as we observe the blind man and the Pharisees take opposite stances.

The story reflects the disputes between John's church and the Synagogue circa A.D. 90–95. Originally Christian Jews remained attached to the Synagogue, but gradually this changed as disputes regarding who *more* possessed the light, Jesus or Moses, began to rage, as was reflected in the last discourse. The blind man will be excluded from the Synagogue because he is a disciple of Jesus. Yet John shows him going more deeply into revelation regarding Jesus, not less, while the Synagogue slips further into darkness because of its rejection of

Jesus, and in the end is judged spiritually blind.

The Jewish mentality at that time would judge this man as a sinner *because* he was blind, but Jesus repudiated the theory of sin as a cause of disability. Rather this man's condition gives Jesus an opportunity to do a work "of God" and for God. And in so doing He will show what *real* sin is, from God's point of view, namely the refusal to accept that God's Light has come into the world *in* Jesus, but some prefer darkness to the light (3:19). The blind man will see because of the light, while the Pharisees who say they have light will not see at all. The sightless, sinful beggar, who is ignorant of the Law of Moses, shows that he has the necessary requirements for entering the Kingdom of God, whereas the Pharisees, who have all the advantages of being devout descendants of Abraham, leaders of the Synagogue, learned in the Scriptures, lack the one thing necessary, which is openness to *more* revelation from God. In clinging on to their little light they lose *the* Light, which is very sad. Because they then belong to those who refuse the light they try to extinguish it, but do not succeed either with the blind man, or Jesus, or later the Church.

After the last discourse Jesus had to hide Himself from the leaders who wanted to extinguish the light. Now He finds a man who needs the light because he was born blind, and chooses him to demonstrate who He is, namely God's light-with-us, *Ego Eimi* with us as the Beloved Son. Jesus must continue to "*carry out the work of the one who sent me*; *the night will soon be here when no one can work.*" He will continue to give His life-giving light and life to those who are open to it. His Hour is coming soon and then He will no longer be in their midst, but as He associates His disciples in this work of giving life to the world He looks ahead to after His death. There is also a hint that John is speaking to his Church to continue to testify to Jesus as long as they have time. The "night", the end of all things, is coming, when they will no longer be able to do this work, so they are urged to persevere as long as possible.

Recalling the first creation in Genesis 2:7, where God fashioned man from the dust of the earth, and then breathed life into him, Jesus made a paste of His spittle and clay, rubbed it onto the man's eyes and ordered him to go to Siloam and wash it off. John tells us that Siloam means "one who is sent", which is Jesus' own designation for Himself. So is this man about to reflect something important about Jesus? Siloam somehow reflects the mystery of Jesus as the Well of Living Water, the source of salvation for all (see also Isaiah 12). In obedience to the word of God through Jesus, the man went and washed and SAW! Like the father of the sick boy, this man discovered that his obedience released the power of God to work for him, to give light to his eyes. As he stumbled away the re-creative power of God began to operate, and so began his own personal journey into the Light, in the deeper sense, at that very moment. Psalm 13:3 had been fulfilled in him: "*Give light to my eyes or I will fall into the sleep of death.*'

Reactions to the miracle were varied: his friends and neighbours realized that something had happened. They questioned him regarding his identity and he made an astonishing reply. He said: "*Yes*, I am *the one*." He said "*Ego Eimi*"! John has now catapulted us into a new revelation that is more amazing than anything he has said before. It is one thing for the Beloved Son to claim to be the I AM, but can a disciple of His say this too? Can the "I AM NOT" of the sinner be transformed in the life-giving waters of Siloam to become another "I AM"?, a replica of the Beloved Son? (see Galatians 2:20). Is this what Jesus is offering in all those marvellous symbols of life, light, bread, new wine, birth from the Spirit? It is staggering to realize that He wants to make of *us* beloved sons and beloved disciples. That we, too, will be "sent" into the world on mission, to give life and light and life-giving bread, sent by the Beloved Son even as He was sent by the Father. But this anticipates the second half of the gospel.

A little secret into understanding John is to realize that whatever section we read in this gospel, we grasp the points being made if we constantly flash back to what went before, and flash forward to what is still to come. Each chapter reflects both ways in its varied revelations.

In the interrogations that follow we watch the healed man grow ever deeper in his knowledge of Jesus. Initially he understood Him as *the man called Jesus* who happened to have healing powers. Once he was brought to the Pharisees, however, pressure was put upon him to declare who Jesus *really* was, for unfortunately the healing took place on the Sabbath, and on that day it was forbidden to knead material for ointments, or to initiate a healing that was not a life-and-death matter. So in the eyes of the legalistic Pharisees Jesus is a Sabbath-breaker, not a light (5:10-18). They are not prepared to look at the fact that Jesus does exactly what GOD does on the Sabbath, namely, give life. Rules have been broken and that's it. For John's readers it is frightening to discover that *Ego Eimi with us* is being accused of darkness! John has told us in verse 3 that this healing was a work of GOD, and one of God's works.

Typical John, the story becomes intricate now as the Pharisees, who do not realize that they are sinners, accuse Jesus of being a sinner, and also throw the healed man out because he has been a sinner since birth as far as they are concerned. We know that sinners should not judge each other because their judgement will not be true, it will not reflect reality as it really is. All judgement must be left to the Son who judges correctly (5:22, 8:15–16, 9:39). The healed man is not impressed by the Pharisees' reasoning, and when asked, he declared Jesus to be a prophet, that is, one who has come from God with a mission and a message for Israel.

Still refusing to acknowledge the light, and the works of

light, the leaders find a way out by refusing to believe that the man was blind in the first place, so they sent for his parents, who, because of their fear of being cast out from the Synagogue, will not speak up at all. They are victims of human respect (5:44), and so forfeit their opportunity to make a profession of faith in Jesus. When asked the crucial question: *whence* came their son's sight? they should have declared that it came from "above", from the realm of Love with its limitless possibilities: that God is at work in Jesus, but they do not. They fail to be true disciples.

This reflects the problems in John's Church, at the end of the first century, as exclusion from the Synagogue was not a problem in Jesus' time, nor in the early days of the Church. The Acts of the Apostles witnesses to the fact that the early Church in Jerusalem frequented the Temple and observed all the Jewish customs. But now, after the destruction of Jerusalem and the persecution of Christians by the Jews, the time has come for the separation of Church from Synagogue. Some Christians are tempted to go back "to Moses", and some want to be secret disciples of Jesus while staying in the Synagogue. These are reflected in the parents, who because they want to remain in the Synagogue, are tempted to deny Jesus by refusing to proclaim that *He alone* has the fullness of light. John wants them to take courage and not be afraid to be cast out, as the healed man will be, for they lose nothing in going over to Jesus.

By contrast the man professes Jesus openly and bravely no matter what the cost, so he is offered as a model disciple to John's Church, and to us. He is now put under oath to declare that Jesus is a sinner because He has broken the Sabbath. The man simply reminds them of the *fact* that he has received life-giving light. Becoming more aggressive, the Leaders demand another recounting of the miracle even though they have heard it several times before. Ironically the man understands this to be enthusiasm for the truth and asks them: "*Do you want to become disciples yourselves*?", which is obviously the point at issue, but it only brings abuse upon him and a declaration that *they* are disciples of Moses.

They are sure that God spoke through Moses, but they confess ignorance of Jesus, and "*from where*" He comes. It is strange Moses' origins are clear to them but not Jesus', even though Jesus had not been bashful in declaring His origins (John 5–8). Strange too that Moses' signs revealed that God was with him, yet Jesus' signs reveal nothing to the Pharisees about whose side Jesus is on. Yet it is the sign that leads the healed man to look into Jesus' origins, and thus he grows deeper in understanding as *even he* realizes that the Messiah will be a mysterious person whose origins will be unknown, one who will open the eyes of the blind (Isaiah 29:18, 35:5, 42:7).

He reasons that if Jesus were not FROM GOD (so, he knows where Jesus comes from), He would be as useless to solve the world's problems as the rest of them were. His bravery, as an uneducated man, in standing up to the powers-that-be is admirable, and reminds us of the Apostles before the Sanhedrin in Acts 4:13. Obviously we are looking at an example of true discipleship, where the person is unafraid to witness to Jesus under any pressure, and is prepared to take the consequences, just as Jesus Himself bore witness to the Father before all Israel and took the consequences in His death.

After the man had been thrown out Jesus went looking for him, as it is not easy to cope with losing one's religious heritage and all the tradition that goes with it. John wants to say that in losing the Synagogue the man has found the Son of Man, the Saviour and Judge of all the world, who will be revealed fully in His Hour. In a moment of exquisite beauty the man humbly asks Jesus for the identity of this Son of Man, addressing Him as *Kyrie*, which can read "Sir" or "Lord", "*Lord, tell me who He is so that I may believe in Him.*" And Jesus tells him that He is that person. At once the man said: "*Lord, I believe*", *AND worshipped Him*. He has now come fully into the light, and worships in spirit and in truth. The I AM NOT has been transformed into a small "I am" in Jesus. He is a new creation in Christ, as Paul will teach later (see Galatians 6:15, etc.). This "nobody" in the eyes of the world has gone further than anyone else yet in responding to Jesus.

The true judge gives His verdict now. His light discriminates between those who accept God's offer and those who reject, thus the blind will see and those who say they are sighted spiritually become more blind. The Pharisees understood that this judgement showed up their innermost thoughts and motives. Unless they change they will remain in their sin (8:23).

Chapter 10

"I AM" is Shepherd of the Flock

This chapter both continues the dialogue following the healing of the blind man at Tabernacles, early in October, and prepares us for the revelations at the feast of Dedication in mid-December. Its teaching spans what has gone before and prepares for what is to come. Verses 1–21 are, therefore, transitional. Jesus is about to contrast Himself with the false shepherds of Israel, who have rejected rather than saved the man who received his sight. Now this man, and all whom he represents, will discover in Jesus, not only the light, but also a Good Shepherd who will give them access to the Father and his Divine Life.

The Feast of Dedication, which was also a feast of lights, was set up to commemorate the re-dedication of the Altar of the Lord after its desecration at the time of the Maccabees (1 Maccabees 1–4). It was a relatively new feast (circa 165 BC), which incorporated readings about good and bad shepherds (Ezekiel 34), due to the fact that the high priests at the time of the Syrian invasion had betrayed their high office (2 Maccabees 4). But the shepherd theme has deep roots in Israel's history. The Patriarchs, Moses and David, were some of their most famous shepherd-leaders, both national and spiritual. Ezekiel's prophecy regarding the shepherds and sheep, made during the exile, reflects the corrupt shepherding of the nation before that time (Jeremiah 23:1–6; Zechariah 11:4–17, 13:7). Because of all this, expectation had grown that one day the Lord Himself, the Chief Shepherd, would take a more immediate and personal hand in leading the people, in the New Age (Psalm 23: Isaiah 40:11).

The language of Ezekiel's prophecy is so close to what John wants to say that it will interpret it for us: "*Son of man prophesy against the shepherds of Israel . . . Disaster is in store for the shepherds who feed themselves! Are not shepherds meant to feed the flock? . . . you have sacrificed the fattest sheep, but failed to feed the flock . . . you have ruled them cruelly and harshly . . . For lack of a shepherd my sheep have been scattered . . . I am against the shepherds. I shall take my flock out of their charge . . . I myself will take care of my flock . . . I shall rescue them . . . I will pasture them . . . I shall look after the lost one . . . I shall be a true shepherd to them . . . So they will know that I, their God, am with them . . . and you, my sheep, are the flock of my human pasture, and I am your God.*" (Ezekiel 34:1–31).

The Model Shepherd (10:1–21)

Having proclaimed Jesus the fulfilment of the Temple and all of its feasts, we now hear John declare that the True Shepherd of Israel has come to fulfil all that was said of Him. The present leaders at the time of Jesus, and John, were following in the footsteps of the false shepherds before them, by preventing the people from penetrating the Light that God had sent them. Jesus is the Beloved Son who has come to take the leadership of the Flock himself. The former blind man may be separated from the Synagogue and its leaders physically, but in doing so has found *the Shepherd of Israel*, and thus he experiences all that God has promised to His people Israel.

Although we are familiar with the use of parables in the Synoptics, we meet them here for the first time in John. He uses several together: Jesus is both the Shepherd and the Gatekeeper. Leaving out the parable story itself, John uses the images involved to reveal Jesus further to us. That of the gatekeeper comes from the normal practice of keeping several flocks in a common fenced corral at night, with a trusted sentry to guard the sheep from thieves. If the sentry was alert the thief would have to climb over the wall to get at the sheep, which would not give him access to many, but if the sentry was untrustworthy, then the lives of all the sheep were at stake. This gatekeeper was the only access to the sheep by the shepherds, and also the only access to pasture for the sheep, so he was a vital person. He was the only way in and out.

Each morning the shepherds arrived to claim their sheep, whom they would call by name. The sheep were trained to listen to the voice of their own shepherd, and to respond to the name given them. He then led them out to pasture. If he were a good shepherd he would lead them to good pasture and care for them well, but a hireling, who was only interested in his day's pay, might neglect the sheep, who would then be in danger, not only of sickness and death from lack of food, but also from predators.

Jesus begins by declaring that it is *really true* that He alone can give us access to the sheepfold. He is the gate to the Kingdom of Heaven. There is no other way. In fact those who attempt another way are the thieves of the parable. It is marvellous to contemplate the "I AM" standing between earth and heaven, the connector between the realms of "above" and "below", being God-with-us for the sheep-fold, and our intercessor with God on the "above" side, thus the fulfilment of Jacob's ladder in 1:51. The two sides of "I AM" are seen here, the God-side and the human-side, and how He functions for us. As Gatekeeper, He also has an in-and-out function, as one side of the gate looks into the sheep-fold and the other out to the world. On the inside He is the good shepherd who brings the sheep to pasture, and on the world side He is their protector from the enemy. It is thus that John introduces us to the revelation of Jesus' Love, which will be the main theme of the second half of the gospel. He is there *for us*.

The great problem of the Temple is now solved, that of access to God. All sheep (believers) have that access through Jesus, who is the ONLY shepherd of the Flock. In His flock everyone has, not only access, which was unheard of for ordinary people in the Old Testament, but a one-to-one intimate relationship with the shepherd. This fulfils Psalm 118:19–20, where the psalmist asks God to "*Open for me the gates of saving justice, I shall go in and thank the Lord. THIS IS THE GATE OF THE LORD where the upright go in.*" Each one of the sheep *follows* the shepherd as a good disciple, not as one of a crowd, but as one who is personally known, called, and loved. As good disciples they follow only the teaching of their master, and do not listen to the stranger's voice which would lead them astray. The ordinary people of Israel were not following the leadership of the Pharisees, as was demonstrated in the blind man standing up to them and challenging their interpretation of the Law.

The leaders, who are now wilfully blind, do not understand what Jesus is saying. Referring not only to them, but probably to false messiahs as well as revolutionaries who claimed to "save" Israel, Jesus said they were all thieves and bandits. Belonging to the realm of "below" they could only operate this world's principles, and this was no solution, as was seen in the fact that the ordinary people saw through their egocentric motives, and did not follow them. A heaven-sent solution was given through Jesus, who offers complete security to the believer. He has come, not to further His own interests, but to give, not only the fullness of life, but the fullness of God's life to them. Unlike the present shepherds in both Jesus' and John's time (which would include the idea of false leaders in the Church too), Jesus works solely for God and the flock, who mean so much to Him that He will lay down His life for them (Acts 20:28–30; 1 Peter 2:25, 5:1–2).

As the Father shows His Love by sending His Beloved

Son (3:16), so the Son indicates the depth of His love by His desire to make the ultimate sacrifice for them. His disinterested love with its total self-giving is His answer to the cry of the needy, and it contrasts sharply with the normal practice of worldly leaders. John has told us here the meaning of Jesus' death. He wants us to penetrate its mystery. It will seem to those "below" to be the triumph of darkness, but those who have had their eyes opened will recognize it as a work of sacrificial love accomplished in tandem by the Father and the Beloved Son for love of the flock.

Within the flock each person experiences the same intimate loving knowledge with Jesus as he does with the Father. This word "knowledge" implies a deeply personal, committed relationship where one is both known and loved, where the "I AM NOT" of the believer can be transformed into the "I AM" of union with the Beloved Son in everything, where the disciple experiences the overflowing love of Jesus and His endless giving, just as Jesus does with the Father. Thus He passes on to the "sheep" His own privilege of Sonship, because He loves them so much. Unlike the Jewish leaders who limit their flocks to race and national descent, Jesus intends bringing the whole gentile world within His fold, so that they will experience all of God's unfathomable Love. Like God in the Old Testament, Jesus is the one who unites the people of the world as the People of God (Ezekiel 34:2–6: John 11:52).

The power behind the realm of "above" that unleashes God's limitless Love into the unbelieving cosmos in order to draw it to new life, is the laying down of one's life for others in pure love. The Father gave us everything He had in Jesus. Jesus gives us everything He has in this outpouring of sacrificial love. The gift of His life is given with the freedom of a lover who delights to give life to the beloved. And for Jesus it is part of the expression of His love for the Father. Besides, this giving is neither failure nor loss. His death begins an ascending movement that rises from the "lifting up on the cross" to the lifting up in glory. When He picks up that life again, He unleashes all the power of the realm of "above" to His disciples to go into the world to transform it for Him. Thus Jesus becomes the eternal Shepherd, *Ego Eimi with us*.

The Jewish leaders present cannot see the eternal Shepherd in Jesus, and accuse Him of being insane and possessed. Judging by human standards and expectations they dismiss Him, not because of any intellectual inability on their part, but because of their unwillingness to respond to the challenge inherent in the teaching for them. The Good Shepherd will not force Himself on anyone, though He is willing to *give light* to any of the blind who want to see.

The Feast of Dedication (10:22–42)

The scene now shifts to winter and the last part of the trial of the Beloved Son in John. We find Jesus in the Temple sheltering from the cold east wind, as He walked up and down the lovely Portico of Solomon, which formed a part of the covered cloisters that decorated the outermost section of the Temple. As we have seen at the other feasts, Jesus claims to be the fulfilment and replacement of this one also. This feast celebrated not only the consecration of the Temple as a whole, but of its altar in particular. Jesus having already revealed Himself as the New Temple, now claims to be the altar of God too.

The ever present leaders gathered around to press Jesus to confess openly whether he was the Messiah or not. Obviously they have given thought to His claim to be the shepherd of Israel, and this term would remind them of the expected Davidic Messiah who would be the king-leader in the political sense of ruling the nation. The Synoptics put this question on the lips of the High Priest during the passion (Mark 14:61; Luke 22:67). They demand that He drop the use of parables and speak plainly. Jesus treads carefully in His reply, as He wishes to speak of Messiah in very different terms to theirs, far beyond their earth-bound limited ways.

Jesus again refers to His works as His witness, as well as all the previous statements in this gospel which explain the mystery of His person. The problem of their incomprehension lies in the fact that they refuse to become His sheep, born from "above" and on the side of truth, literally "of God", as He is (8:47, 18:37). They look and listen only on the political and material level so they do not "see or hear" on Jesus' level, where He could liberate them. By contrast Jesus gives eternal life to those who believe in Him. As the model shepherd, Jesus declares that they will never be lost, which means that the enemy will never succeed with anyone truly given to Him. The Father, who has supreme power over humankind, is the one who works in tandem with Jesus, and therefore Jesus can offer eternal security to the believer (Wisdom 3:1; Isaiah 43:13).

The total unity of Father and Son is now revealed. "*The Father and I are one.*" Jesus came from the Father (8:42); is loved by the Father (3:35); is in intimate relationship with Him (8:55, 10:15); He is the sent one who does only what He sees the Father doing (5:19); He was taught by the Father (8:28) and receives all His power from Him (5:22); He does the will of the Father (4:34, 6:38). These are all aspects of that claim to be ONE with God.

This response of Jesus meets with violence again as they fetch stones to stone Him, because this time they HEARD the implications of the claim, and they wish to kill Him, not for good works but for blasphemy. This is the first time John mentions the actual charge for which the Sanhedrin handed Jesus over to be crucified. They said, in their darkness, that He was making Himself equal with God, but Jesus never *made Himself* anything! He always said that the

Father was everything and the source of all His good. Jesus is not a man making *Himself* equal with God: He is rather the Divine Word who has become flesh to bring us God's word (1:14).

In reply Jesus cited Psalm 82:6, a text which shows that Israel had considered her judges, who were the shepherd-leaders after Moses, to be "gods" because they had the God-given privilege of ruling the nation as His appointed instruments, to bring both proper judgement as well as God's word to the people. If these ordinary, sometimes corrupt, and mortal judges could be given such exalted titles, then surely *God's Word Incarnate*, the shepherd and judge of the world, should be allowed to be called Son of God, since that is His reality. There is irony in Jesus telling them that scripture cannot be cast aside. It is God's revealed word. Yet these people are in the very act of casting aside God's final revelation in the Person of The Word, Jesus. How can the words of the Book compare with The Word Himself? (Letter to Hebrews 4:12–13).

Unknown to them, Jesus is the consecrated Son, the HOLY PLACE where God is to be encountered in the New Age, the very altar of God. They knew that to defile the altar was to defile God, but do they know that to deny Jesus is to deny the Father of Israel, the very Source of their religion? As consecrated Son Jesus does the work of His consecrated Sender, with His authority and power, what they understood to be the role of an ambassador. The works reveal the workman to anyone who will reflect. Jesus then makes a pathetic appeal to them at least to give Him credit for doing the works of God, even if they don't like Himself as a person. "*If I am not doing my Father's work, there is no need to believe in me; but if I am doing it, then even if you refuse to believe in me, at least believe in the work I do; then you will know for certain that the Father is in me and I am in the Father.*" But they are blind and cannot "see" the light, so they again try to extinguish it. How sad!

The rejected Beloved Son now leaves Jerusalem until the appointed time, and he goes back to where His ministry started on the far side of the Jordan, where John the Baptist had been baptizing. There as at the beginning, many ordinary people "came to Him" on both levels, first to see and then to stay as disciples.

Chapter 11

Life to Man / Death to the Son of Man

We now approach one of the peaks in this gospel, as John seeks to illustrate Jesus' power to give life in this last and final sign that provides a transition from the Book of Signs to the Book of Glory. The raising of Lazarus will precipitate the death of Jesus. Lazarus will receive the gift of *physical life*, which though still not in the realm of "above", is so close to it that it forms a fitting conclusion to the ministry of Jesus, and an introduction to His ministry of glory, because it is a prophetic action that anticipates the true meaning of His Hour.

Nowhere else in the gospel do we see John bring together in one incident so many of his statements about Jesus: He is Rabbi (8), Lord (12), Son of God (4), the Resurrection and the Life (25), the Christ (27), the one who has come into this world (27), the Master (29), the man who should die for the people (50), the Beloved Son in communion with His Father (42), and at the same time the human being who can cry at a funeral and really feel for others (33–36). All this is given with the revelation that He had close friends whom He loved dearly, and whose home offered Him shelter, hospitality and love during His stays in Jerusalem. It is worth noting too that His greatest sign was demonstrated on someone whom He both loved and trusted, someone whom John presents as "a" or "the" Beloved Disciple, someone who will allow Jesus to bring him from death to life, both on the level of "below", namely physical life, and on the more important level of "above", that of eternal life. Lazarus is someone who would be "with Jesus" for ever, just as Jesus will be "with" the Father, who will raise Jesus "on the third day" soon.

As usual John incorporates all that has gone before and all that is still to come, to explain fully what he says here. We have just emerged from a discussion of the Good Shepherd who dies and rises for the sheep whom he loves so much. He knows each one by name, and calls them out to find pasture, which means that he leads them to eternal life. Here we see one of his sheep has been snatched by death, the ultimate darkness. Jesus comes to call Lazarus by name out into the Light of Life, out of the clutches of "death" for ever. This is because the "eternal life" that Jesus offers is not just something that *lasts* for ever; it is a *quality of life* that is *indestructible*; which means that "death", both physical and spiritual, cannot touch it. Jesus comes, therefore, to bring the ultimate victory, which is Resurrection life that we, as His loved sheep, enjoy now and for ever.

Jesus claimed that no one could snatch His sheep out of His hand, and certainly not from the Father (10:28–29), yet John is about to show us both Shepherd and sheep in imminent danger of just this! Lazarus is about to die and the Son of Man is about to die. After two arrests and two stonings have been attempted, we know that it is only a matter of time before the authorities "get" Jesus. Are they to be snatched from the Father? This chapter gives the triumphant answer by showing that the shepherd will liberate His sheep from the clutches of death, and then go on to conquer death for ever, thus liberating from its power everyone who believes in Him. Then all will understand this "life from above" for what it really is, God's Life, which transcends everything human, material and transient.

By contrast the realm of "below" has no answer to death. It is a dark mystery better not spoken about, to be avoided and feared. To cause a person's death appears to be victory for "darkness", yet this is the very "weapon" that Jesus and the Father choose to overcome darkness for ever. The darkness had never comprehended the Light, and could not put it out. When Resurrection dawns, God's eternal life and light illuminate our world for ever, enabling anyone who wants to see and live, to do so. Disciples of Jesus will learn to lay down their lives in imitation of their master because, like Him, they will take it up again. So death has lost its sting (see 1 Corinthians 15:35–49; John 11:16, 13:38, 21:19). Jesus, therefore, is not only the gate or door to the sheep-fold, He is also the Gate to Heaven.

The Dead are Called to Life (11:1–44)

As we had two movements in the healing of the blind man, so we have here. Lazarus will be called to live again and the Jewish leaders will decide to kill Jesus. Life for Lazarus means death for Jesus, but ultimately it leads to the glory of God. Jesus has been in Bethany on the far side of the Jordan (10:40, 1:28) and now a letter from His friends Martha and Mary calls Him to the Bethany near Jerusalem.

There is a "call" theme running alongside the "coming out" theme in this chapter: the sisters on behalf of the sick man call Jesus, who comes to them. Thomas called upon the other disciples to go and die with Jesus. The Jewish friends come out from Jerusalem to sympathize with the family, and find themselves called to faith and new life. Martha called Mary to come out of the house to meet Jesus, having come out herself to meet Him outside the village. All this leads to the coming of Lazarus from the tomb at the call of the Beloved Son.

One cannot miss John's cry to everyone to listen to this call of Jesus, first to come out of the death of our sins, to come out from the realm of "below" into the New Life which is the realm of "above". If we respond, then John tells us that this gift of eternal life in Jesus is both physical and spiritual, that our rising from our sins now will issue in our physical rising from the dead on the last day. Thus John illustrates the teaching in 5:25–29: the hour is here when the spiritually dead will rise at the call of Jesus, and the physically dead will rise too. So for Christians, to be in the grave or out of it does not matter, because they have this indestructible life that goes on for ever in them. This is why Paul tells them not to grieve at the death of a loved one, like the pagans WHO HAVE NO HOPE (1 Thessalonians 4:13–18).

A very significant message was sent to Jesus: *Lord, the man you love is ill*. Lazarus is a beloved disciple, therefore he represents all Christians for whom Jesus will die to give them life. These friends of Jesus know Him very well (15:15). Love is the essence of the Christian life, and the only acceptable motive for our actions. It is the principle that Jesus turns into a command (13:34), demanding an exact photocopy "as I have loved you" from them. To appeal to His love for His disciples is to touch the softest core of His being. On receiving the message Jesus responds as He did in the case of the blind man: God's glory will be revealed through this if only they will trust the Son of God to work. Jesus knows that it is not Lazarus' death that will issue from this, but His own. It will herald HIS HOUR, whereby He will glorify the Father by His sacrificial death, and the Father will glorify Him in the Resurrection, which will reveal finally who He is. This is mystery, not tragedy.

John emphasizes Jesus' love for the family at Bethany, in case we would misunderstand His deliberate delay in coming to them. The sisters have asked for a healing but Jesus wants to give them a resurrection because, as Paul says in Ephesians 3:21, God always wants to do more for us than we ever ask or imagine. So He waited until the third day to decide to go to Judaea, which is dangerous for Jesus now, and the disciples are afraid. Unknown to them Jesus is, in fact, going up to Judaea to die (Mark 10:32–34), and only He can decide when the time is right, so He calms them with a parable on travelling in daylight when it is safe (Jeremiah 13:16). There is the usual double strike here, for the disciples are eternally "safe" if they walk by Jesus' Light. They will not stumble unless they fall into darkness again. On the human level Jesus is free until His Hour. Their shepherd-leader does not stumble, but walks steadfastly towards His Hour.

Jesus announces the sign: "*Our friend Lazarus is at rest; I am going to wake him.*" These words sent a quiver of delight into all creation. Death is no longer the end of everything. It is only "sleep" or "rest" until the Beloved Son calls one to the Resurrection Life. Of course the disciples do not understand. How could they, when Jesus was not yet risen Himself? So they thought that Lazarus must have taken a turn for the better, and his ability to rest would allow the curative powers of the body to work, so why go to Judaea when it was so dangerous? In the realm of "below" this makes sense, so Jesus calls them back up to His level and announces that Lazarus is dead. Now the unbelieving cosmos would say there was no point at all in going! Jesus explains His delay in that this miracle, more than the others, will strengthen their faith and reveal to His disciples who Jesus really is.

Thomas, one of the Twelve, whose voice has not been heard before, but whose adoration of Jesus will bring the gospel to its climax, now speaks up. He suggests to the disciples that they should go to Judaca and die with Jesus. Like other speakers in this gospel, he only partially comprehends what he is saying. Thomas must die to self, to that egocentric principle of the realm of "below", if he is to rise to New Life fully (Mark 8:34–35). Only Jesus can give him this spiritual "awakening", as only Jesus can give him the eternal awakening, after he has followed his master later in laying down his life for his brethren (20:28).

On arrival Jesus found that Lazarus had been buried for

four days, so this can in no way be written off as a resuscitation rather than a resurrection. Lazarus must have died the same day as Jesus received the letter, for He delayed two days and travelled another two days. Since Bethany is only two miles from Jerusalem, the many Jews who came to sympathize with the sisters from there were ordinary people, not the leaders, so they will not be hostile to Jesus. Martha went out to meet Jesus while Mary sat at home. This is the usual description of the active Martha and the contemplative Mary (Luke 10:38–42).

The meeting between Martha and Jesus has the several levels that we found in the interrogation of the blind man. Part of what is said is a pre-resurrection story, intermingled with post-resurrection Christian faith in Jesus. Remembering this helps to understand the apparent contradictions in Martha's statements. At first she complained that if Jesus HAD (past tense) been here the present tragedy would not have happened. Then she looks into the eyes of Jesus and her faith soars ALMOST to the point of believing in the possibility of a resurrection: "*. . . but even now I know that God will grant whatever You ask of Him*." Looking at Jesus, and listening to her heart, Martha expresses the hope that EVEN NOW, when it is beyond hope, Jesus will DO SOMETHING. This resembles Mary at Cana speaking to the waiters after Jesus had refused to act (2:5). Responding to this new openness in her, Jesus announces that her brother will rise again. Martha immediately falls back into "head knowledge" as she remembers the doctrine of the resurrection on the last day, which is so far into the future that it is no challenge in the here and now (see Mark 12:18; Acts 23:8; Daniel 12:2).

Martha's inadequate faith is challenged by Jesus who announces: "*I AM the resurrection. Anyone who believes in Me, even though that person dies, will live, and whoever lives and believes in Me will never die. Do you believe this*?" Martha had not realized that the gift of Life that conquers death is a PRESENT reality in Jesus. What she expects on the last day IS HERE, NOW. Anyone who has received from Jesus that life which is begotten by the Spirit of God will survive death, both physically and spiritually. They outlast death because this life of Jesus is indestructible, and it overcomes spiritual death because it is eternal.

Belief in Jesus (chapter 3) releases a person into this life-giving relationship. Jesus is the source of life now, and of life hereafter for all His beloved disciples. Martha's reply sounds much more like the faith of John's Church in its post-resurrection knowledge, than that which Martha could reach before it, as we will see in a moment when she tries to prevent Jesus from going into the tomb. Her reply here, that "*I believe that you are the Christ, the Son of God, the one who was to come into this world*", has such revelation in it that it would invite Jesus to go to the tomb. The beloved disciples later understood that *on that day* they were privileged to stand beside the Messiah, the one whom all Israel expected, but who surpassed all expectation by being the Son of God, the one who is the source of all life, spiritual and temporal; the Father's presence in our midst.

Anticipating the resurrection accounts, Martha, who has accepted Jesus as the Resurrection and the Life, must go to tell the good news to Mary, who comes out in response to the call of the master, so that she, too, may come out into this new dawning light. Their Jewish friends accompany her and thus find Jesus. Mary's response to Jesus is the same as Martha's, blaming Him for not coming in time.

Jesus' response to her is very different to His response to Martha. He is angry and upset. John says that Jesus "was greatly distressed", and that He cried. The Greek word he uses implies that Jesus was upset in the very core of His being. He was deeply troubled. Scholars have had a field day in trying to interpret Jesus' distress here. Typical of the gospel it will be on two levels. Jesus really feels for His friends in their mourning and shows His own loss by tears.

On a deeper level He is probably very disappointed in the inadequate faith of those who are closest to Him. If THEY have not penetrated the mystery of His person, then who will? He knew that the crowds still wanted miracles with no challenge to change or grow, and He cried tears over Jerusalem for the same reason (Luke 19:41–44).

Here the Jews who see Him cry wonder why He could not have PREVENTED this man's death, but Jesus came to CURE death, and to transcend it. From their standpoint the ultimate in love would be to prevent death, but the Love that originates from "above" has a more wonderful solution – resurrection. Yet in confronting death, Jesus confronts the whole realm of darkness, and its originator, Satan, who has brought nothing but pain, sickness, destruction and death into the world. Here His anger is directed to His enemy, whom he will meet in single combat in Jerusalem. His agonized compassion moves Him to raise Lazarus now, and raise all men later.

As Jesus went towards the tomb Martha tried to prevent Him, because Lazarus had been four days there. It was the belief of the rabbis that after three days a body could not be resuscitated, hence John has repeated that Lazarus was BEYOND the help of this world. Martha reacts, as she is asked to "do" the work of believing in the practical sense. Jesus replied: "*Have I not told you that if you believe you will see the glory of God*?" She must come on to the higher plane that enables God to work, otherwise she will stay on the level of those who do not believe and do not see the glory of God manifest in their lives, because their unbelief prevents it.

Jesus ordered them to remove the stone which protected the outside of the tomb. In raising the dead there was something for them to do and something for Him to do. They must remove the barrier to Life, then He will call the person into life. His Light will go into that tomb of rotten death, and from its depths of darkness and despair will come forth new life. This anticipates the work of the Believing Community later.

Jesus, who has been accused of blasphemy for having made Himself equal with God, humbly addresses the Father in prayer, showing that He is fully submitted to Him as a Beloved Son, but also as one "sent" by Him to perform His works. It is those around who need this assurance, not Jesus, who could have performed the miracle without the prayer. His prayer is loving and full of confidence, expressed humbly and with gratitude. As one who lives in union with the Father (10:30), and who only does the Father's will (4:34, 8:29). This same confidence, for the same reason, will be demanded of the beloved disciples later (14:12–13, 15:16, 17: 23). Jesus rejoices in the fact that the Father is about to reveal Himself in an irrefutable sign that will lead many to faith.

The prophecy of Isaiah (49:9) that the Lord would one day call the prisoners from their prisons and those in darkness to come out and show themselves, finds more than fulfilment here as Jesus speaks into the darkness of death, the ultimate prison, and commands it to give up its prisoner. The voice of the Son of God has gone forth to do its creative work as it had done at the dawn of creation (1:1–5). "*Lazarus, come out*!" He cried; and if He had not named the victim, all the dead who had died since Adam would have come forth in joy, since that was what they were waiting for, resurrection day!

Since death is the prison that resulted from sin, this calling forth is the ultimate in *forgiveness*, which means to let the person go free to begin a new life (the Samaritan woman and the adultress). When Lazarus came forth, obviously miraculously, since he was bandaged from head to foot, Jesus commanded those around to "*Unbind him and let him go free*". Again the preview of the Mission for the beloved disciples. Jesus asks them to share in His work of unbinding people by their forgiveness (20:23), thus setting them on the new road to *real life*. Lazarus has become a symbol of the fully redeemed person living the new life.

This greatest of Jesus' signs reads like a preview of His own Resurrection, which will be "on the third day" after "darkness" will appear to have taken Him captive. The two days' delay after His death will be very difficult for His disciples to handle. They will be in mourning and in tears, as the two women are in this passage (Mark 16:10), unable to believe fully without help from Jesus (20:4–10, 20). Here the Jews think Jesus should prevent the death, and there they will demand of Him to come down from the cross to prevent His own death (Matthew 27:40–44). There will be a tomb with the stone rolled away, and grave cloths, but unlike Lazarus Jesus will come forth to the New Life of the Resurrection clothed in the Glory of God, not needing the grave cloths of earth. It will be a sign totally *from above*.

Lazarus still had the grave cloths of earth clinging to him, illustrating the temporary nature of the gift in a few extra years added on to his life, whereas Jesus broke into the eternal timelessness of God. In both we have mention of the head cloth which was tied under the chin to prevent it sagging in death. Lazarus still wore his, whereas Jesus removed it without help. The freedom of Lazarus' resurrection, wonderful though it is, cannot be compared to that of Jesus, who could pass through doors and walls, having broken through the barriers of time and space.

Reaction: Death for Jesus (11:45–57)

The reaction to Jesus is still the same: some of the Jews who came to the funeral believed, but the others went to report to the Pharisees what Jesus had done. This resulted in a meeting of the Sanhedrin where Jesus was tried *in absentia*. Since the meeting was secret the *real* accusations against Jesus are spoken. First, that Jesus' signs were so great that

His popularity was drawing the people away from the present leaders: what would happen if all the people went over to Jesus? Mark 15:10 agrees here with John that it was out of jealousy that Jesus was handed over to be killed. Second, that Jesus' success with the populace was a matter of concern for the Roman Governor who was continuously having to quell Jewish uprisings. The Sanhedrin is concerned in case the Romans find an excuse to destroy the Temple and the city, a disaster which must be averted at all costs. Their political expediency backfired, as the death of Jesus did not prevent the Romans from destroying Jerusalem and the Temple in A.D. 70.

John claims that the High Priest, Caiaphas, unknown to himself, actually prophesied. Jewish rabbis associated the gift of prophecy with the office of High Priest, so this would not surprise the early Christians, for whom this would be familiar. Although operating from the realm of "below", God still used him because of his exalted office. Reading his prophecy from "above" one feels very sorry for this man, who was so blind to the fulfilment of all that he hoped for, both for himself and for the nation. Jesus' death *would indeed save* Israel, but not politically. He was not to die *in place of* Israel, but on behalf of the *true Israel*, those who believed in the Word of God and the Messenger of God, who were part of the Flock of Jesus. As their true Shepherd, He would gather the dispersed children of Israel into his flock (see Isaiah 11:12; Micah 2:12; Jeremiah 23:3; Ezekiel 34:16).

It was even more marvellous than Caiaphas declared for "*. . . Jesus was to die . . . not for that nation only, but also to gather together into unity the scattered children of God.*" He could not have grasped that Jesus' popularity would not only not diminish, but actually increase with his death! And the long-term effect of it would be the conversion of the Gentiles (12:32; 1 John 2:2). The Sanhedrin did not know, as did the Samaritans, that Jesus was *the Saviour of all the* *world*. Ironically the *end* of Jesus heralded the *beginning* of the world's salvation. Not only that, but the end of Jesus would herald the *end of the Temple*, for He was its replacement (2:19–21). In Him the prophecy concerning the Temple as a house of prayer for all nations (Isaiah 56:7) would find its fulfilment. It would be to the hill of Calvary, spiritually and temporally, that the pilgrims from the ends of the earth would come from this time onwards (Zechariah 14:16; Isaiah 2:2–5).

The decision of the Council to kill Jesus meant that Jesus had to go away to Ephraim, near the desert for safety.

The Great Passover Approaches (11:55–57)

The die is cast now and the Hour of Destiny approaches. The sense of apprehension that will cover the next few chapters is already upon us, that awesome sense that something too great for us to grasp fully will occur, and we are not sure how we feel or should act. The order for Jesus' arrest has gone out from the Sanhedrin, so that the early prilgrims arriving for Passover wonder whether Jesus will have the courage to come in face of this new turn in events. As they prepare to celebrate the great events of their deliverance from slavery, they have no idea what is about to occur in the final confrontation between Jesus and the authorities. Jesus is a wanted man, but an unwanted Saviour.

Chapter 12
Darkening Skies

As the time of Passover draws near we again observe two opposite movements: Jesus' enemies gather in hate, while His friends gather in love. The two realms of "above" and "below" are seen to be poles apart in action, intention and outcome. The raising of Lazarus unites the powers of "darkness" against Jesus, and, determined to kill him, they look for their opportunity. Remembering back to 1:29, 36, *we know* that the Lamb of God is about to be sacrificed at Passover. All the saving grace the people pray for at Passover will be given from the place of execution out on the lonely hill of Calvary, which they despise. They celebrate life and liberty, and Jesus is about to give eternal life and true liberation.

Anointing for Burial (12: 1–11)

At a dinner provided by His friends in Bethany, which included the disciples as well as Lazarus, with Martha serving at table, Mary publicly anointed the feet of Jesus (Matthew 26:8–9), attesting to her great love and gratitude for the life restored to her brother. Using the most costly ointment, fit for the burial of a king, costing three hundred days' wages, she lavishly anointed *the feet* of Jesus, wiping them with her long hair. It was the custom to anoint *the head* of a living person. Anointing the feet was done for the dead, so Jesus proclaimed that Mary had unconsciously acted prophetically in preparing His body for burial.

Her great love for Jesus was directed towards His great act of Love for all humankind. She, like all the other beloved disciples, knew that Love could be repaid by love alone, as her gesture indicates. And this love for Jesus and the brethren could not be calculating. It had to be great-hearted, as Jesus' was, and hers was. John says that the house was filled with the odour of the ointment, just as Mark 14:9 testifies that her story of unstinted love would fill the Church for all time, since it would be recounted for all future disciples as an example of how to respond to God's Love. Jesus' heroic act of love on Calvary will fill the universe with the odour of His love, so that all races and peoples would glorify God as a result.

Not everyone present was on the level of Love. Viewed from "below" this was a waste, for three hundred days' wages would really help the poor. But the protester is Judas, who was in charge of the finances of Jesus' group, and instead of giving to the poor (who, according to Deuteronomy 15:11, should be provided for all the time as a matter of justice) he used the money for himself, with no regard for justice at all. Coming events will show that he not only stole the money in the kitty destined for the poor, but his betrayal of Jesus seeks to rob Him of His life.

His cold, calculating action reveals the absence of love, that very special mark of the realm of "above". If Mary is a model of a true disciple, Judas is the opposite, one who no longer believes in, or loves, Jesus. Instead of defending Him in time of need, he will find himself on the side of "darkness", and will co-operate in His death. Thus Judas is the great example of the failure of grace to transform someone who did not co-operate with it (17:12).

Lazarus now finds himself caught in the tension between God and Israel, as his resurrection was the centre of controversy. It was sensational news to the people, who flocked to see this man come back from the abode of the dead, something Moses never did. Such was the response of those who saw him, that crowds were coming to believe in Jesus at last. The reaction from the Sanhedrin was to decide to kill Lazarus also, although he was so newly returned from the grave. Poor Lazarus!

The insanity of sin and "darkness" is shown by the fact that the Sanhedrin gave no thought to the idea that if Lazarus had come back once, he might come back a second time in an even more sensational way, showing that he was unkillable. And what about Jesus? If He restored another man's life, could He not restore His own? Better not to touch what you cannot handle, but they will not hear this, in their determination to destroy both the Giver of Life and the recipient. So they go down in history as people who unknowingly helped God to do what they did not expect Him to do, and missed their opportunity to share in His gift.

Behold, Your King Comes (12:12–19)

The following day a great crowd of those in Jerusalem for the festival gathered branches of palm and went out of the city to welcome Jesus formally into their midst as King. This was the normal welcome given to a victorious king on his return to the city after political or military victory (1 Maccabees 13:51). As they advanced they sang Psalm 118, which begs the Lord to come and save them. Hosanna means "save us now", so the crowd unconsciously made the right request of Jesus, as that was the very reason why He had come.

"They took branches of palm and went out to receive Him saying: 'Hosanna! Blessed is He who is coming in the name of the Lord, the King of Israel.' " This Psalm, which was written for the Feast of Tabernacles, was also used at Passover, and it spoke of the stone rejected by the builders becoming the keystone, which would be a marvellous work of God. This finds its fulfilment in the rejection of Jesus by the leaders of Israel, who, unknown to them, is their true king. The psalm cries out for the saviour God had promised them, and when He comes they will process with palm branches even to the altar with Him. This crowd in Jerusalem use the right psalm but with the wrong meaning, for they address Jesus as the earthly King of Israel. They misunderstand Jesus' kingship, just as the crowd did in Galilee after the multiplication of the loaves (6:15). Neither group penetrated the sign to what it signified.

Jesus sought to dispel this misunderstanding by a prophetic action which the disciples understood only after the resurrection. He found a donkey and mounted it as the procession went on, while those who had seen the Lazarus miracle witnessed to everyone. It was a noisy scene of singing, witnessing and palm waving. Riding the humble donkey, which was a symbol of peace, not war, Jesus indicated that His kingship was "not of this world" (18:36). It was from the realm of "above" and those in the old order would have no ability to discern it.

Jesus' entry into Jerusalem was the fulfilment of prophecy, for Zechariah 9:9 had spoken of a victorious king who would come to Jerusalem riding humbly on a donkey, one who would bring peace to the nations, indeed to the ends of the earth. God's concern then was for all nations, in contrast to the people's narrow nationalistic hopes. Zephaniah too (3:16–20) spoke of the great day when the Lord God would be in the midst of His people as a warrior-saviour, and His coming would be to renew them with His Love. The emphasis in Zephaniah is on the Lord rescuing the needy, as we saw Jesus do with the Samaritan woman (chapter 4), the cripple (chapter 5), as He fed the hungry (chapter 6), rescued the sinner (chapter 8), and the blind man (chapter 9), looked after His sheep (chapter 10) and raised Lazarus (chapter 11).

For those who have eyes to see, the Lord God *has* come to them, in Jesus their king and saviour. He has come to fight the definitive battle with evil in order to give them, and all the world, New Life through His victory. The

Pharisees, seeing His immense popularity, unconsciously prophesy that the *whole world* will go after Jesus. They are right, for the worldwide Mission will begin very soon, and there is nothing they can do to stop it.

Yet mystery surrounds this humble king, whose only anointing was the anointing for His death. The only crown He wore was a crown of thorns, which He accepted in order one day to give His disciples a crown of glory. His kingly robe was given in mockery, but He won the robe of righteousness for us. When He stands before THIS SAME crowd a few days later, dressed as their king, they will shout for His death: such is the realm of "below". Everything about Him and His kingdom takes its authority, power, and its scope of activity, from "above".

A Son's Agony (12:20–36)

Among the pilgrims who flocked into Jerusalem for the Passover were some Greek Gentiles who had come to believe in God. They approached Philip and asked whether they could "see" Jesus. Both Philip and Andrew went to Jesus with this request, which drew from Jesus the dramatic statement: "*Now the hour has come for the Son of Man to be glorified*." It is as if the coming of the Gentiles is the sign Jesus has been waiting for, to trigger off the solemn events of His Hour. The Pharisees have declared that the whole world is running after Him, and here the gentile world requests entry into the Kingdom of God, because in John to "see" is to believe in Jesus, with all its consequences for salvation. Matthew's gospel puts the approach of the Gentiles at the very beginning (chapter 2), while John puts it at the end of Jesus' life.

The two disciples Philip and Andrew were prominent at the sign of bread (chapter 6) when Jesus indicated His desire to feed the world. Now they are to the fore again as Jesus approaches the fulfilment of His promise, when "the world", represented by these Gentiles, comes to Him to be fed. But how will it come to pass? Jesus says: " . . . *unless the wheat grain falls into the ground and dies, it remains only a single grain; but if it dies it yields a rich harvest.*" In this beautiful parable Jesus explains that He must be ground to powder in order to make this bread which can impart eternal life. In yielding up His own life He will give life to the Church, the new community of beloved disciples. Nature is full of this death-and-life mystery. There can be no harvest unless the seed is put into the ground and yields up its life. Its death is *the source* of the harvest, and Jesus has already revealed that His disciples will reap a harvest they have not sown (4:34–38). Paradoxically Jesus' death is the means of gaining life, so to refuse to die would be a refusal to bear fruit (Isaiah 53:10–12, 55:10–11).

This holds true for His Beloved Disciples also. To release in them the life from "above", they must put down the egocentric principle, so that in the here and now of time they can live the New Life. If they refuse to put down the egocentric self they will never realize their true selves. Death and life must be continuously at work then if we are to reach our full potential, even on the natural level, for selfishness is destructive there also. This John expresses in those enigmatic words: *Anyone who loves his life loses it; anyone who hates his life in this world will keep it for eternal life* (Mark 8:34–38; Matthew 16:24–26).

Those who wish to be true disciples will SERVE JESUS just as He has served His Father, and they will FOLLOW Him through this life of service to the laying down of their lives in death to realize the harvest in the next generation, so that sower and reaper can rejoice together in the Father's Presence (4:36). Christians must walk the same path as Jesus and come to the same glory. Just as Jesus and the Father are one (10:30), so Jesus and His Church are one (17:23: Acts 9:5; 1 Corinthians 12). If the disciples are *to follow Jesus*, then He is on His way to public rejection, unfair trial before the representatives of both Jewish and gentile worlds, and a public execution at the hands of both. In His Resurrection the disciples will see the unlimited power of God that is unleashed through one seed dying out of love.

Nevertheless such a giving is costly on human nature, for Jesus as well as His disciples, and He becomes deeply troubled at the approach of the confrontation with Satan. This is John's equivalent of the Synoptics' "Agony in the Garden", but John gives it in broad daylight and during the ministry, as he did with the trial, and the temptations. Jesus is tempted to choose another way, but realizes immediately that THIS WAY is the Father's will, and submits to that.

"*Now my soul is troubled. What shall I say: Father, save Me from this hour? Father glorify Your Name!*" This is the moment of destiny when, as the Lamb of God, He must decide to take on board "the sin of the world" in order to release the power of the Spirit into the cosmos (1:29, 33, 19:30, 20:23). He must go down into the depths of the unbelieving world and conquer it with His immense Love! Can He shoulder the pain and distress and lostness of a universe without God? He is tempted to ask His Father to save Him from it. Instead He realizes that the mystery of Light and darkness, love and hate, belief and unbelief, life and death must meet in this ultimate confrontation that will glorify the Father. So Jesus asks the Father to glorify Himself through this Hour, which will look so meaningless to blind eyes. Crucifixion will not LOOK LIKE a death of perfect love, humility and obedience. Those of us who are privileged enough to see it from the perspective of the Resurrection can penetrate its mystery and glorify God too.

The Father replied from heaven: "*I have glorified it, and I will again glorify it.*" Jesus' submission met with reassurance from the Father, but those around thought it was just a clap of thunder, or an angel speaking to Him, although one would wonder how these could be confused. Perhaps John is saying that the people were vaguely aware of the conversation between Father and Son, and remembered that God had spoken on Sinai in the thunder, and that angels had conversed with Abraham. Whichever way it is, we are told that Jesus has already glorified the Father in His sign ministry, and He will glorify Him again in His Hour, which will be judgement for the world, that unbelieving mass of humanity without God and without faith in Jesus' divine power to give life. It is Satan's judgement too, for He will be driven out of a world where He claims lordship as the "prince of this world".

The final answer to those Greeks who approached Him (and whom we have probably forgotten!) is that it is only in the mystery of Jesus' being "lifted up" from the earth that He will draw all nations to Himself, making them into one sheepfold under Himself as shepherd. The crowd misunderstands Him, for they heard that the Messiah . . . *would remain forever* (Isaiah 9:6; Psalm 45:6, 89:3–4; Daniel 7:14). They do not realize that Jesus will "dwell" or remain for ever with His disciples in His risen life. So He asks them to believe while there is still time. The hour of darkness is fast approaching when their opportunity to believe will have passed. Then in a dramatic gesture, Jesus hid Himself. The light is fading and night is closing in.

Conclusion to the Ministry (12:37–50)

The Light of the World has gone from their sight now. The next time the crowd will see Jesus He will be a Suffering Servant (Isaiah 49:1–7). Since they have not discerned Him either as Messiah or the Light, neither will they "see" the lowly servant of the Lord. Evaluating the effects of the ministry, John pessimistically states that Israel had not changed towards those whom God has sent her. Her whole history is one of rejecting the prophets. The miracles of the

Exodus had not led the people to put their trust in the Lord, or to walk a life of faith (Deuteronomy 29:2–3). The nation consisted of a few real believers and a vast miracle-hungry crowd, just as this gospel portrayed.

Their refusal to accept the grace offered hardened their hearts, until complete blindness set in. Isaiah's prophetic ministry began with a vision of God's glory, and also an assurance that Israel would not listen! Jesus' ministry fulfilled and surpassed that of Isaiah, yet the response was the same. Isaiah had foreseen that the one who would eventually be "heard" would have to give His life as a ransom (Isaiah 53). Was this what John meant by Isaiah seeing Jesus' glory? That the suffering servant would triumph through His suffering?

. . . this was to fulfill the words of the prophet Isaiah: "Lord, who has given credence to what they have heard from us, and who has seen in it a revelation of the Lord's arm?" Indeed they were unable to believe because, as Isaiah says again: "He has blinded their eyes, He has hardened their heart, to prevent them from using their eyes to see, using their heart to understand, changing their ways and being healed by Me." Isaiah said this because he saw his glory, and his words referred to Jesus.

The mystery of the deliberate blindness of Israel is now revealed, and John concludes the Book of Signs on a note of challenge. Many among the leaders DID believe in Him, but would not admit it. As this appears to be a contradiction of 7:48 we realize that John is speaking of the situation in the latter half of the first century when many priests had come to believe but wanted to stay in the Synagogue (12:42–43; Acts 6:7). So Jesus ends His public ministry with a reminder that anyone who has REALLY "seen" Him has seen the glory of God on the face of Jesus Christ. Such a one will remain faithful to His word and know that the Father speaks through Him.

Part Two

The Book of Glory Reveals the Beloved Disciples

Introduction

The public ministry is over now, with its atmosphere of confrontation and tension, as Jesus tried (in vain for some people) to reveal that His coming was the fulfilment of all their hopes and dreams for the Messiah. For the next few chapters we find ourselves in a private room with Jesus and His disciples, in the warm atmosphere of love and fellowship. But it is not all cosy. Tension exists even there, and a vague feeling of apprehension and fear in the expectation of alarming events to come. The two levels of "above" and "below" are present also, with Judas acting as the agent of the realm of evil and the disciples not understanding the full import of what Jesus reveals to them.

The context is that of the final Passover in Jesus' life. The gospels differ in the details of events, but the main points are similar. For John, Jesus dies on the eve of Passover at the very moment that the paschal lambs were slaughtered in the Temple, and He is buried BEFORE the holy day which began at sundown (19:42). In the Synoptics all the events of Holy Thursday and Good Friday take place between the beginning of Passover and the following evening, with the problem of so much activity occurring on such a major holy day.

The reason for both presentations is to stress that Jesus is the Paschal Lamb who is taking away the sin of the world (1:29, 19:14, 36). The references to hyssop and unbroken bones also recall the Passover (19:29, 36; Exodus 12). So for John, Jesus is not only the Shepherd but also the sacrificial Lamb; not only the altar, but also the sacrifice and the priest (19:23), making Jesus the complete replacement of the Temple and ALL its activities and feasts, since He is Temple, altar, priest and sacrifice. But only those firmly established in the realm of "above" will penetrate this mystery on Passover Day.

Likewise John does not present the institution of the Eucharist within the Last Supper as do the Synoptics. He transplanted it into the discourse on the Bread of Life (6:51–58), giving us instead the scene of the footwashing which obviously comes from an independent source of tradition. John is also unique in giving the long farewell discourse of chapters 13–17. It represents the last will and testament of the Messiah to His Believing Community of beloved disciples.

There is precedent for this in the Old Testament, which presents the farewell discourses of Jacob (Genesis 47), Moses (Deuteronomy 32), Joshua (Joshua 23), and David (1 Chronicles 28). The New Testament gives something similar in the eschatological discourses of Jesus in Matthew 24, Mark 13 and Luke 21, while Acts 20 presents Paul's farewell to the church at Ephesus. From this evidence one would expect Jesus, as a great leader, to give final instructions to those who will carry on His work when He has departed.

The general pattern of the Book of Signs was to present a discourse AFTER the sign, but here in the Book of Glory the opposite happens, as Jesus must explain the coming events BEFORE they happen, so that the disciples will be able to survive and their faith grow. What their eyes will tell them on Calvary will be only partially true. They must see the whole movement of Jesus being lifted up on the cross first, and then lifted up in glory. It is His return to the Father that is all-important, for it will prove His DESCENT from the Father.

Chapter 13

Footwashing: The New Service

The Footwashing (13:1–20)

Before the festival of Passover Jesus knew in His heart that the time had come for the REAL Passover, when He would return to the Father through His death and resurrection, thus inaugurating the New Exodus of the New people of God, from the realm of "below" with all its sin, unbelief and destructive forces, to the realm of "above", where Love and Grace and fraternal unity reign. Love was the motivation behind the Passover, on God's side. Unbelief, malice and jealousy are the motives on the world's side. Jesus' gift of Himself in death is an expression of His perfect love for His disciples (Galatians 2:20; Romans 8:35, etc). . . . *having loved those who were His in the world*, [*He*] *loved them to the end*. His was love taken to its absolute limits, and also to the very end of His life, a love so God-like and pure that it would release His disciples from the slavery to sin and the ego-self to become copies of Himself, living on His level of self-giving love.

They were at supper. This is the love-feast of the Kingdom of God that Christians were to celebrate for ever as a memorial of His love and also a participation in its saving effects. The whole of the farewell discourse takes place in the context of this meal, as the early Christians understood the Eucharist to be the Sacrament of fraternal love and unity (1 Corinthians 10:14–17, 11:17–34). Yet the evil one is at work even among these privileged followers. Judas, because of his unbelief and sinfulness, became the agent of the devil (8:44, 12:31, Luke 22:3; 1 Corinthians

2:8), who is the unseen power behind all the unbelief and sin of the cosmos. Because of this Judas will do the unthinkable, which was to hand over the Messiah to torture and death.

Jesus knew that the Father had put everything into His hands, and that He had come from God and was returning to God . . . Everything depended on Jesus' perfect love for the miracle of the true Passover to be accomplished. Everything depended on His perfect obedience to His Father too. If He does not go through with this sacrifice, the Devil will remain in charge of the unbelieving cosmos as its "prince". Jesus could have dealt with His deviant disciple, but instead He accepted His betrayal in order to deal with the REAL enemy, so that the world would be released from his vice-grip, if they wished. He KNEW that it WAS a Passover, not a "death", that the marvellous power of God which flowed from Him in His ministry would now flow into the entire cosmos carrying it towards its destiny, and He was assured of victory in His return to the Father.

As soon as the unseen forces that would bring about his crucifixion had been set in motion, Jesus got up from His position as head of the table, and carried out a prophetic action that would explain both the meaning of His death, and also the type of service that His beloved disciples were to give when He was departed from them. . . . *He got up from table, removed His outer garments and, taking a towel, wrapped it round His waist; He then poured water into a basin and began to wash the disciples' feet and to wipe them with the towel He was wearing*. John uses the same verb for Jesus' "laying down" both of His clothes and His life (*tithenai*) (10:11, 15, 17, 18), and for the "taking up" both of the clothes and the life (*lambanein*) (13:12, 10:17, 18), hence the action denotes His death.

The footwashing was the duty of a slave or a servant (1 Samuel 25:41). But the problem of the disciples wanting to be the first and the most important (Luke 22:24–27) pertained even now, so that there was no one to do this menial task necessary at the beginning of the Passover meal, which was eaten in a reclining position. They do not yet understand that a king is still a king when He kneels at their feet, and that His humility only serves to show that His kingdom is "not of this world". It operates on the principles of love and humble service, which the disciples find difficult to grasp. The principle of the egocentric world they are emerging from is that of power politics and manipulation of people. These two orders clash in the footwashing.

Jesus wants them to know the power released through powerlessness, the life that is released through the death of "self". They too must lay aside their desires for position, power and importance in the worldly sense, in order to be free to raise the dead in His name. If they are still caught up in the world's game, they will be powerless in the spiritual sense, which spells failure as disciples. Jesus' action seems to have rendered them speechless, as we have no reaction from anyone except Peter, who realizes that this service should be the other way round, and is embarrassed by it.

After all the trouble Jesus has gone to, to reveal Himself as the great I AM, it is a shock to see Him kneel before them as a servant! Is all the glory and splendour of God wrapped up in this humility? Is God's greatness manifested in this service that nobody else wants to do? Like the cosmos they still do not understand that the Kingdom of God operates on love alone, that love is the power, and humble service the position they must hold before the world they will serve (1 Timothy 5:10).

He came to Simon Peter, who said to Him, "Lord, are you going to wash my feet?" Jesus answered, "At the moment you do not know what I am doing, but later you will understand." Before the passion Peter can only see the washing of his body, but after the resurrection he will realize that it was on Calvary that Jesus did the humble work of washing our sins away (1 John 1:7; Revelation 7:14; Letter to the Hebrews 9:22, 10:22; Titus 2:14, etc), and that Christians will experience the effects of this in the washing of Baptism, and the cleansing from sin in His forgiveness (Acts 22:16; Titus 3:5, etc).

If Peter does not agree to this he puts himself outside his inheritance as a disciple of Jesus. To enter God's Kingdom means allowing Jesus to wash away our sins and elevate us to the level where God's love operates in our lives. Peter over-reacts then and asks for a complete bath. To be cut off from Jesus is intolerable, but this thinking is earthly. Peter is unable to receive and be vulnerable before Jesus and the disciples. He would rather fight WITH Jesus and die FOR Him, but now he hears that the opposite is the fact. He needs Jesus to fight and die for him, to raise him from the level of "below" to the realm where Jesus can give him a part in His mission to all the world, where his influence will be felt down the ages, for this love is divine, and therefore unlimited in its scope and fruitfulness.

It requires humility to receive real love as well as to give it, as we saw Jesus receive the love of a devoted disciple in the "bathing" of His own feet in 12:3, so He gives it to His own beloved disciples here. Both "bathings" were associated with His death. Peter and the others have been cleansed by Jesus' Word already, and now they are being fully cleansed by His blood shed for them.

"*I have given you an example so that you may copy what I have done to you.*" When Jesus had dressed and returned to His place as the Master and Lord, he asked for a "photocopy" of this action in his community of beloved disciples. Disciples normally copied their masters in everything external, including dress, walk, accent, teaching, etc. Jesus asked for a "photocopy" of an INTERNAL attitude towards everyone, within and without the community.

They were to be motivated by love and humble service publicly and privately, and it is not inconsistent with high office, since their Lord and Master set the standard. They have a pattern of behaviour put before them which will bring great blessing in the DOING of it, as this obedience would release the power of "I AM" to transform them into images of the Beloved Son (2 Corinthians 3:18, etc). He is preparing to send them into the world as His messengers, just as the Father had sent Him, so they need to be exact copies of Him as He is of the Father.

But all of them were not cleansed by the footwashing or the death of Jesus, and all of them will not go forth in His name. Judas is the exception, the one who remained untouched by Jesus' Word, the one who has not entered into or accepted Jesus' love. He had not allowed himself to be freed by Jesus' forgiveness, so he remains in the world of power and manipulation. In his blindness, he will carry out an action that was foreseen by the prophets (Psalm 41:9), that a close friend would "lift up his heel" in an action of contempt against Jesus. Jesus forewarns the others so that their faith will be confirmed in its fulfilment. They will know that "I AM" submitted to betrayal, humiliation and death for love of them. Thus John's Christians must not be confused if there are some "Judases" in the late first century either, as Judas is the model of all who fail to respond to Jesus' love.

The Betrayer and the Beloved Disciple (13:21–30)

What to become and what not to become are shown in the contrast between the Beloved Disciple and Judas, for they are seen at opposite ends of the spectrum of discipleship and relationship to Jesus. Only three of the disciples present are mentioned, all of whom bore a special relationship to Jesus. They were placed near Jesus at the table because in a reclining position there was very little room for movement. One reclined on the left arm with the body stretched out, so only movement with the right arm was possible. This places Judas on Jesus' left as a special guest, and John on his right where he could lean back on Jesus' breast, and all three at the head of the table. Peter, some distance away, had to sign to John to ask Jesus to reveal the culprit.

However, placing at table is not the issue. It is one's relationship to Jesus that is all-important, as we shall see. Jesus was troubled again (*tarassein*), the same word that John used as Jesus stood before the tomb of Lazarus. This "troubling" has to do with His confrontation with Satan and death, as we saw in 11:33 and 12:27, and it has to do with the traitor who will set these events in motion. He reveals him now as one of the Twelve! This disturbs the disciples, who look searchingly at each person at the table for the first time. Maybe they had no need to look at each other deeply before, but after this they will need to examine one another for fear of the wolf turning up in sheep's clothing (Acts 20:29–30).

The one closest to Jesus finds out who the traitor is. Real closeness to Jesus is not physical but spiritual, and it gives discernment to the disciple who, like his master, will be a copy of the one who sent him, and be commissioned authoritatively to speak in His name. He will "know" Jesus just as Jesus knew the Father. The two options for disciples are clear now: to become a photocopy of the Beloved Son or of His betrayer, as the spirit of the world creeps back into the heart. There seems to be no halfway house.

In response to the request of the Beloved Disciple, which was prompted by Peter, Jesus gave Judas the morsel. This was a gesture of love to a special guest (see Ruth 2:14). From the troubled depths of His heart Jesus offered Judas another sign of His undying love, yet Judas, who has stopped loving, accepted the bread but without changing his resolve. This was the moment of judgement for him as he chose the darkness over the light (3:16–21). Satan, that enemy who has opposed God from the beginning, now enters Judas as his "prince" or master to guide him towards destruction, for he was a murderer from the beginning (8:44). Jesus, who is in control of his destiny, now asked Judas to leave, as He will not reveal the true depths of His love until He is alone with His faithful companions. *It was night* in every sense. It was now the appointed time for the Lamb as well as the powers of darkness (9:4, 11:10; Luke 22:53). Jesus knew that the Father had put everything into His hands, EVEN SATAN, whose darkness He will overpower by His undying light and love (1:5). The long night of the passion will have a wonderful dawn on the first day of the New Era on Easter morning.

The Command to Love (13:31–38)

Now that Judas is gone the atmosphere changes, and Jesus addresses His beloved disciples as His "little children", words that make sense in the context of the Passover meal, where each group must celebrate as a family, where the leader is the "father" and the others are his "children". The beloved disciples are being formed into Jesus' new family (Mark 3:31–35). Then He launches into the final discourse that makes available NOW the glories of the HOUR, a discourse that surpasses in nobility and majesty the most marvellous discourses of His ministry. The latter were addressed to hostile audiences, whereas this one is for "His own" whom He is preparing for His impending departure.

Already He has passed into the timelessness of God, and so he speaks to them both "in time" and "out of time", mixing the two dimensions as He prepares to let go of the limitations of time to pick up the inrush of timelessness in His resurrection. He speaks to them at the last supper and also from heaven, and addresses Himself to the faithful disciples around the table then and now, for His beloved disciples would have to master how to live a heavenly life on earth if they were to be His photocopies.

The essence of the new life is love, God's Love flowing into us to transform us, and then going out from us to form community. It is the ONE command that Jesus gives His beloved disciples, and it is to be the hallmark of their existence, the point of recognition by outsiders. In the context of the Passover meal (Luke 22:11) which celebrated the glories of the Exodus and the making of the Covenant on Sinai, Jesus – who is about to inaugurate the new Covenant in His own blood (Luke 22:20; 1 Corinthians 11:25), a Covenant which will fulfil the prediction of Jeremiah 31:31–34, which proclaimed that all would be given an intimate loving relationship with God – gave them this one command which summarizes the Ten Commandments of the Old Law.

The Old Law commanded love, with all the heart and soul, mind and spirit, to be given to God (Deuteronomy 6:4–5), and love to be given to one's Israelite neighbour (Leviticus 19:18) as well as to the stranger who dwells with you (Leviticus 19:34), but Jesus raised the standard very high as He asked them to love, not only God, but each other, as He has loved. The love Jesus has for His followers is not only affective but effective, as it brings about their salvation. The distinguishing mark of God's Love in the Covenant is the fact that it is offered to sinners, people who are unworthy of such love, and it is given spontaneously and freely, as Jesus' love is. Their love for one another will, therefore, have to be sacrificial, open-eyed to the faults of the one loved, laced with forgiveness, up to and including the laying down of one's life for the brethren. It is this mutual self-giving in love that will mark out HIS disciples from all others (Acts 5:12).

Simon Peter reacted to the knowledge of Jesus' departure, by wanting to know just where His master was going that seemed to imply that he could not go with Him. Jesus' reply was a veiled reference to Peter's own martyrdom, when he would not FOLLOW Jesus now, but later. Peter protests that he would lay down his life for Jesus, not realizing that he has not yet been tested. Only in the test will he know definitely what he is able to do in his own strength, and relying on THAT he will deny his master that very night. Only when Jesus has been lifted up in glory will He "lift up" this disciple to the level of "above" where, relying on God's grace, he will follow his master in life and in death, and become a worthy copy of that Image of Love.

There is pathos in this dialogue as Peter does not estimate correctly either his own strength or the difficulty of following Jesus. It is easy to talk of Love, but it spells death to the ego self to live it, and may cost us our lives too. Neither does he realize that following Jesus unto death involves a struggle with Satan and the powers of evil. Jesus said: "*Now you cannot follow Me where I am going, but later you shall follow Me.*" Now, this very night, Jesus will go into battle with the powers of evil and overcome them. Only then will it be possible for Peter and the others to follow. In fact after the resurrection Jesus will ask Peter to take on the shepherding of the flock, a role that will end in his laying down his life for his master.

Chapter 14

The New Dwelling Place

The last chapter gave us the second "beginning" of John's gospel that we wish to consider. In 1:18 we were introduced to the Beloved Son who dwelt in the bosom of the Father for all eternity. This intimacy enabled Him to know the Father's heart fully, gave Him the authority to reveal Him to others, and His surrender to the Father meant that as the sent one He could do the Father's work and accomplish His will on earth. Now in 13:23 we are introduced formally to the Beloved Disciple and he is leaning on the heart of Jesus in a relationship of intimacy and love. The gospel reveals no personal name for this disciple, although he was well known to John's church. As he is the model for all disciples he is introduced only as the Beloved Son prepares to depart.

The group Jesus addresses in His final discourse will become His beloved disciples, photocopies of Himself (hence we referred to them this way in the first half). Therefore each one of them must enter into intimacy with Jesus as He did with the Father. They must come to know and understand Him, and live a life of surrender to His will and His word, so that as His "sent" ones (the meaning of *apostle*) they can speak authoritatively in His name, carry out His mission and do His works. They will be moulded into a Community of Love which will reflect the Trinity in heaven, a community of one mind and heart in surrender to God and to each other, working to bring God's Kingdom on earth.

They will experience the implacable hatred of the unbelieving world even as Jesus did. Thus they can expect persecution, but they will be guided and directed by the Spirit whom Jesus will give them as He departs. All that the Son is in relation to the Father they are to become in relation to the Son, hence Jesus began by giving them the governing principle of His own life, namely Love, which is both His gift to them and His command.

Dwelling Places (14:1–14)

Just as Jesus had "troubled" Himself and shuddered before the thought of the struggle ahead, so now His disciples are perturbed at the predictions of betrayal, of Jesus' departure and of Peter's denial. Jesus seeks to comfort and strengthen them for all that lies ahead. Real faith in God implies real trust and hope, so Jesus asks that as they continue to trust the Father they should also trust the Beloved Son, as they approach their greatest test of faith. It will look as if they have been abandoned from the world's point of view, but in fact Jesus will have gone ahead of them on the New Exodus to make a home for them in the Father's house.

Here we are reminded of Deuteronomy 1:33, where the Lord went ". . . *ahead of you on the journey to find you a camping ground* [literally, "dwelling place"], *by night in the fire to light your path, and in the cloud by day*." In His seeming absence Jesus will be present as their light, and will journey with them throughout the ages, always making a way for them and showing the way ahead, and the place in heaven is assured also. Not only temporal, but eternal security is given them. Their privilege is to be "with" Jesus and the Father in a relationship of special intimacy, both in the here and now of time and also when death comes.

Jesus reminds them that they know "the way" to that place, for Jesus is Himself *the way*. Misunderstanding Him Thomas thinks that Jesus is going away on a journey to another place. He objects that since they do not know

WHERE He is going how COULD they know the way? Thomas is thinking on the level of "below". Jesus must open his eyes to limitless possibilities in the realm of God's Love. So He said: "*I am the Way; I am truth and Life. No one can come to the Father except through me.*" Just as the Father made a way for Israel in the past, so Jesus makes a new way for His followers (Letter to Hebrews 10:19–25). There is no access to the Father except through the Son, since the Son is the New Temple, altar, sacrifice and priest. He is both Shepherd and gate to the sheepfold, through which believers must pass if they are to find the "full life" (10:9–10). He fulfils Isaiah's dream of a new and sacred way that the redeemed would travel on (Isaiah 35:8).

His Way is also the "way of Truth". Since God IS reality, He alone can reveal what reality really is. The Old Testament longed for God to show the "way of truth" to His people (Wisdom 5:6). Jesus has come to show the way OF Life and the way TO Life, the only way of salvation (10:9). His "way" is also the way OF Truth and the way TO Truth, because He is the revealer of truth and life (6:63, 5:24). Jesus is the embodiment of truth and the source of life to His followers. His way, the way of true life, and the true way to find authentic life, includes suffering and death both in the death of the egocentric self and of the laying down of the life for others. Not only will Jesus find the Father when He goes through death, but so will they. If Thomas and his companions have understood this they will realize that to see Jesus IS to see the Father, for Jesus is the revelation of the Father to them.

Philip speaks up for all those who refuse to believe without seeing (20:29) and demands a revelation of the Father – obviously a theophany such as Moses or Elijah had on Sinai. Perhaps through him the early Christians were asking Jesus to reveal His "being with the Father" in some dramatic way? He fails to grasp that the Word of God incarnate is before his eyes, and there is no further need of "spiritual experience" to discern God's presence. Philip should have discerned this long ago as he communed with Jesus on the way, for in seeing Jesus one sees God. As God's "sent one", His special agent, Jesus is to be identified with the One who sent Him, and His works reflect this reality (Deuteronomy 18:18, 34:10–12).

If Philip has not grasped this first lesson, how will he grasp the truth that with the others, he is to be "sent" by Jesus and that together they will form the new Temple (see 1 Corinthians 3:16, etc) that will house the Presence of God? How will he "do" the works of Jesus? Jesus wants them to do even greater works than He did Himself when He stands by the Father in intercession for them. Just as His works were those of the Father, so theirs will be the works of Jesus brought about by the indwelling Spirit (see Ephesians 4:7–16).

Faith will open them up to the flow of God's power to perform mighty works that will be life-giving to others, works that will glorify Jesus, as His works glorified the Father. Like Jesus they will have to re-create heaven in the human heart (15:5; Mark 16:17–18; Matthew 21:21). The thought of doing greater works than Jesus must have been very daunting, especially as they ALSO have the seemingly impossible command to love as He loved. How will they do it? The answer lies in their prayer-life. It is in communion with the Father and Jesus that their requests on behalf of others for Word, Life, Light, Bread, Living Water, etc, will be answered. Their mission of selfless love will be empowered through prayer, and through this same mystery they will be gradually transformed into the image of the Beloved Son (see 2 Corinthians 3:18). The mighty works of believers come out of their prayer of union with the Father and Jesus guided by the Spirit.

Sign of a Beloved Disciple (14:15–24)

The test of the disciple is the same as for the Master,

namely, obedience to God's Will and God's Word (4:34, 5:30, 14:31). In the last unit Jesus made a "believe in me" plea, while here it is a "love me" plea. The Old Covenant demanded love to be given to God, now Jesus makes the same demand (Deuteronomy 6:5). Not that love can be commanded. Jesus is not speaking of human sentiment but of the letting go of the false centre in ourselves to become a self-giving, life-giving person in loving relationship with both God and the community of believers. In fact the command that Jesus gave demands that whatever love is felt towards God is to be shown to the neighbour in works of love. The acceptable sign of love is obedience to Jesus' word. It is love that is eminently practical and concrete, with real fruit.

Even though Jesus in His departure makes great demands on them they will not be without help, for He will send ANOTHER Paraclete to indwell them. The new community of beloved disciples will be on trial before the world after the resurrection, but their defence lawyer is WITHIN them and there is no need for fear. Jesus has protected and defended them up to now during His own trial; the Spirit will continue the work of Jesus both within them and between them and the world. They must accept to lose the physical presence of Jesus to gain the invisible presence of the Paraclete, who will be from now on "God-with-us" (Isaiah 7:14). Only the opened eyes of faith will be able to discern His Presence, so the unbelieving cosmos will neither "see" Him nor "know" Him, but the beloved disciples will experience Him as their everyday reality in delightful mutual indwelling.

Besides, Jesus will Himself return. He has no intention of abandoning them. His return, they discovered afterwards, would be on several levels of reality. First, He would return in the post-resurrection appearances, to a limited number of witnesses. Then He would return permanently in mutual indwelling for all believers; and in

His final coming in the Parousia, everyone would see Him, but in judgement. The other "returns" were to be in love, for those who accepted Him and allowed the miracle of God's love to flow in and through them. The resurrection appearances were to be a special manifestation of His Risen Body to His chief witnesses. Only the inner eye of love would discern the indwelling presence, but both sinner and saint would see Him fully in the Final Glorious Coming of the Son of God.

As Jesus begins to explain the nature of this indwelling and His returns to the beloved disciples, the "trouble" that worried them at the beginning is less now, as the so-called separation of death is perceived to be the beginning of a new mode of living with Jesus which is altogether more unitive than the present one. The new *place* where Jesus will dwell is in the hearts of believers who become *His body* in the world (see 1 Corinthians 12), therefore the New Temple where the Spirit of God dwells, and from which He operates His salvific plan for the world. This is where Jesus will live and the interchange of love will take place. Hence loving the brethren WILL BE loving Him. The mystery of Jesus' going away has brought heaven and earth together in an interflow of life and love: the Father in Jesus and He in the Father: Jesus and His beloved disciples in loving union.

This reveals the mystery of the Mystical Body of Christ on earth. What was hidden from all eternity has now been revealed (see Ephesians 3:9), yet the mystery is only available to those who have opened up to faith and love. As lovers know, the mystery of love only happens when people are truly open to each other, when they live for each other. In the same way the disciples have opened up to Jesus in faith and love, and the indwelling of God is a *present* happening for them. They do not have to wait for death to release them into God's presence. They are already in it.

To be loved by the Father is the ultimate in religious experience, and that is what Jesus offers to those who enter into loving union with Him. Not only that, but Jesus promises to manifest Himself to the inner eye of love, so that the disciple will walk in the present knowledge of the presence of the Risen Jesus. The "other" Judas cannot understand how Jesus could manifest Himself to some and not to others. Obviously He is thinking of a manifestation in the flesh, or else perhaps it is the early Church feeling that life would be easier for them if Jesus showed Himself to His "enemies"? The final return in the parousia is for later; now the return will be in indwelling, and it is imperative that the beloved disciples get on with making a place for Jesus to dwell in their own hearts by internalizing His word.

More Real? (14:25–31)

The disciples wonder whether Jesus is more real now than He would be in His indwelling presence. He assures them that they will be in a better position when the gift of the Holy Spirit has been poured out, for then they will have their teacher within them, enlightening and instructing, and giving them understanding regarding Jesus Himself and the deeper levels of His teaching. It is the function of the Holy Spirit constantly to bring to their minds all that Jesus taught them, so that there is no fear of any of it being lost.

Besides, they will have peace, one of the great messianic gifts, to strengthen them. Unlike the world, which claims to have peace in the absence of war, this peace is a dynamic gift of God enabling the possessor of it to endure conflict, suffering and death with equanimity. It is a synonym for interior happiness and contentment, which the Old Testament knew would be the Messiah's gift (Psalm 29:11, 72:7, 85:8, 119:165; Isaiah 9:6).

Armed with the gifts of peace and of the Spirit, there is no need for fear as Jesus returns to the Father, and the disciples begin their mission to all the world. If they really understood, they would rejoice in the return of the Son to the Father's side, whence He came, and whence He will send the Holy Spirit upon them. Time is short, and Jesus is inwardly aware of the approach of the Prince of this world, thinking he can destroy the Beloved Son. But Satan only has whatever power God permits him to have (19:11), and that does not allow him to have any hold on Jesus. What neither the devil nor the unbelieving cosmos will be able to grasp, is that the surrender of the Beloved Son to all that the Father permits in terms of suffering, will serve to demonstrate to the world the singular obedience of the Son, who showed His love for His Father by perfect obedience to His will. "*. . . the prince of this world is on his way. He has no power over Me, but the world must recognize that I love the Father and that I act just as the Father commanded.*" And the Son asked the same sign of love to be shown by the beloved disciples (14:15, 23).

Chapter 15
The True Vine

To explain the relationship between the beloved disciples and Himself in the New Age about to dawn on Easter Day, Jesus chose the well known image from the Old Testament of the vine and its branches. Israel as a nation had been chosen by God as His "first-born son" among the nations (Exodus 4:22). Those who partook of the Covenant were the "sons" of God (Psalm 82:6), so Israel and its members were referred to as "son" and "sons". What was said of the one pertained also to the other, so what the prophets addressed to the nation was equally addressed to the individual.

Using the same imagery as John, Jeremiah 2:21 says that God had planted Israel as a choice vine of sound stock, yet it turned out to be a degenerate plant. Other prophets corroborate this view (Jeremiah 5:10, 12:10–11; Ezekiel 17:5–10, 19:10–14; Psalm 80:8–18; Hosea 10:1). Isaiah spoke of Israel as a vineyard where the Lord was lovingly at work as the vinedresser (5:1–6). It is interesting to note that here Israel is called "My beloved", as Jesus is about to address His disciples now. Yet God's beloved of old had produced sour grapes instead of good fruit, thus bringing judgement on the vineyard. Judgement meant tearing the vineyard down and burning it (Isaiah 27:2–5), for the vine was needed only for fruit-bearing, its wood being useless except for making fires (Ezekiel 15:1–6).

The image of the vine or vineyard had actually become a symbol for the nation of Israel in its call to be God's beloved. The huge golden vine which stood before the Holy Place was one of the glories of the Temple, and the vine symbol was used on coins at the time of the Maccabees. Unfortunately almost every reference to Israel as the vine or vineyard speaks of God's disappointment with His people's response to His grace. Finally, about a century before Christ, Sirach 24:1–22 identified Wisdom with the vine that would bear fruit, and John has a theme running through his gospel that Jesus is this wisdom incarnate among us. In Sirach's text, Wisdom declares that those who eat and drink her will never be hungry or thirsty again, as we heard Jesus say in chapters 6 and 7.

Jesus has been talking of "indwelling" in the last chapter. Now He wants to explain the nature of this mutual indwelling, so that the disciples will understand that the incarnation continues on in them as branches of God's vine. They are to learn that just as He "externalized" the Father's presence for them, so they are to externalize His risen presence in the world after He has been lifted up. He will be truly living on in them, as the Father was truly living in Him. Now we see that the mystery of "*The Father goes on working and so do I*" (5:17) is to continue, as Jesus will go on working in and through the community of the beloved disciples (Mark 16:20). In death, Jesus will be no more separate from His followers than the Father was from Him. In this way the vine will bear the fruit that God expects, and then both Father and Son will be glorified.

The Real Vine (15:1–17)

Israel knew that the nation as a whole was God's choice vine, even though it did not live up to the Father's expectations. Speaking from the level of "above" Jesus now reveals that "I AM" is the true vine. The New Israel is Jesus Himself. Those who are part of it are also part of Him, and both are born from above. John has gone to great trouble to tell us that Jesus replaced not only the Temple of Israel but also all of its great feasts and sacrifices. Now we see that the Beloved Son also replaces the "son-nation". Christianity is a person, not an institution. This new living organism is the REAL vine, the one of the Father's perfect planting, and it will bear fruit for Him, thus fulfilling God's greatest expectations for Israel. The Beloved Son will do for the Father what the son-nation failed to do.

In the miracle of the bread Jesus offered REAL food and REAL drink in His body and blood. At Tabernacles He offered REAL living water; for Lazarus He gave REAL life, just as He really transformed the sick and the sinner. Now He offers the REAL environment where we can live and grow to the fullness of our capacity, while carrying on the Son's mission to save the world. It is in union with Himself, and with each other, just as He found the fullness of life in union with the Father. The Father is the "director" of this new organism, seeing to the health of the whole, by making sure that the branches are fruit-bearing.

There is no choice for a disciple about whether they will "remain" with Jesus on the vine or not. The alternative is death, just as it is for an arm separated from the body. There is no life for the beloved disciples outside the life of the vine, because Jesus is the source of life (5:21–26, chapter 11). They are as totally dependent on Jesus for life and a continuance of spiritual nourishment as a branch of a tree is on the parent plant. Cut off from the sap the branch automatically dies, not because of judgement, but for lack of nourishment. Jesus not only calls us into life (chapter 5) but sustains that life in us on a daily basis, so the disciples must live in constant openness to God's operations in their lives, and let His Word become flesh in their daily experience, as the sap flows out to every tiny branch of the tree.

John is giving this to us on two time levels, before and after the resurrection. Before the event it is instruction for the vine: afterwards it also offers explanation as to why some branches, like Judas, were eventually cut off.

Branches that had once been alive could die, and then for the sake of the rest of the living tree they had to be lopped off (see 1 John 2:18–19). When Old Israel became degenerate the vine itself was torn down, here the vine will survive because of the presence of Jesus and His Spirit, so only the individual branch is lost (17:12).

Even healthy branches need pruning, is the next sober revelation. Jesus had already cleansed (the literal meaning of the word used for pruning) the disciples at the footwashing, and they are also cleansed by internalizing the Word of God. This pruning is continuous, involving more growth and greater fruit-bearing. The union with Jesus is neither static, nor theoretical, but involves total commitment and growth, with all the pain that entails. For the disciple, the painful choice is that of being cut back in the pruning or cut off in the lopping. The cutting back, though painful, is life-giving, the cutting off is judgement and death. When Jesus says: "*Remain in me, as I remain in you*", this is no longer seen as a choice, but as a necessity for spiritual survival.

The other side of the coin is that as the disciples remain in Jesus by faith, He remains in them by love and fruitfulness. This mutual abiding is what releases the divine life to flow into us, maintaining life, while empowering us to become life-givers to others. Apart from Jesus, we cannot hold on to a spiritual life ourselves, and we are useless to him in building up the kingdom. There is an end-time aspect to this too, as disciples who fail the Lord entirely will find themselves judged, . . . *these branches are collected and thrown on the fire and are burnt* (Matthew 3:10, 13:30; Mark 9:43).

For the good branch that will remain in mutual abiding with Jesus there will be a life of harmony with His word and obedience to His commands, where that person's prayer-life will be in conformity to the wishes of Jesus' own heart and his or her requests will reflect those of the Beloved Son, and be granted. Nowhere is selfish prayer envisaged as effective prayer. It is prayer that emanates from this union with Jesus that is powerful to move the heart of God. Therefore this prayer-life is part of the whole plan of salvation as the Beloved Son, in the beloved disciples, continues His intercession for the salvation of the world. Thus it is in furthering the mission to all the world that the disciples further the glory of God.

Verses 9–17 put love as the centre of both the mutual indwelling and also the fruit-bearing of the disciples. What Jesus asks of His beloved disciples is to bring forth the divine fruit of *agape*-love, which is impossible to human nature, and therefore to the realm of "below". It is literally born of God. It flows from the Father to the Beloved Son, and through Him to the beloved disciples, then through them to each other and out into the world saving, healing and transforming it. It is the "life from above" that Jesus promised to give, enabling the beloved community on earth to reflect the Community of Love in heaven. Being a disciple, then, means first loving Jesus: "*I have loved you just as the Father loved Me. Remain in My love*" (9–10), then loving one another: "*This is My commandment: love one another as I have loved you . . .* " (12–17), even to the point of laying down one's life (13).

This love, fed by God's powerful Love, finds expression in perfect obedience to God's will and word. It is the inner strength and dynamism enabling us to let go of our ego-self in order to take up our true self and become, in and through Jesus, another "I am" in a relationship of total mutual self-giving in love and obedience. As nothing gives more joy than to live in an atmosphere of love and fidelity, Jesus wants us to experience the celestial joy of a beloved son as we rejoice in our privileged relationship to Father and Son in the Spirit, and our relationships with each other in the Body of Christ. So Love, Joy and Peace would describe the experience of a beloved disciple, qualities that Paul gives as the fruit of the Holy Spirit within us (Galatians 5:22).

The command of Jesus to love is now seen to be vital to the new community, as the source of its life and fruitfulness. This "keeping" of the commandment, and "doing" of God's will involves an active response of the heart, whereby we express in the mundane actions of our lives the pattern of life laid down for a beloved disciple. Thus a "command" is not so much an order as a word of God lived out in action, and this, Jesus says, is the acceptable sign of love to God (see 1 John 2:3–4, 3:22, etc). So the command to love is the pattern of life for the new community.

The model of the relationship between Jesus and the disciples is that between the Father and the Son: "*I have loved you just as the Father has loved me*" (see the diagram). The model of how disciples are to relate to each other is the relationship each one has with Jesus: "*This is my commandment: love one another, as I have loved you.*" This means that relationships among disciples are to reflect the perfect mutual sacrificial self-giving of Father and Son (see 1 John 3:16). The expression of this God-like love is the laying down of life. The Father "laid down His life" in giving us His only Son, who laid down His life in self-giving ministry and then in death for our salvation. This is the model for our self-giving love, service, and martyrdom for His Name.

Jesus, in verses 14–15, calls us "His beloved", His friends. "*I call you friends, because I have made known to you everything I have learnt from My Father.*" The message He brought from the Father was about friendship and fraternal love (12–17). He chose the beloved disciples to be His friends, not just servants, so that He could reveal to them all that was in His heart, as the Father had done for Him. The servant relationship would keep them at a distance from Him and He was inviting them, not only into intimacy with Himself, but with the Father and the Spirit also. This was a unique privilege. Jesus wanted whatever

I:

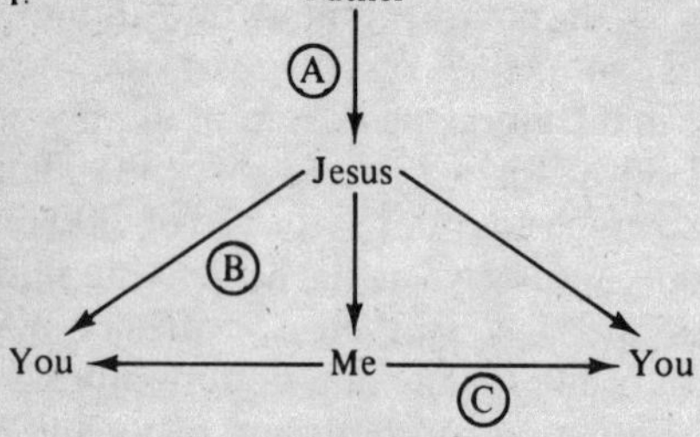

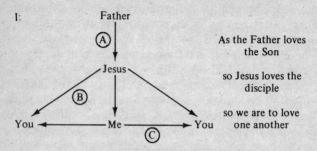

As the Father loves the Son

so Jesus loves the disciple

so we are to love one another

A. The relationship between Jesus and the Father IS *the model* ...
B. ... of the relationship between Jesus and me AND *the model* ...
C. ... of the relationship between the Beloved Disciples.

II:

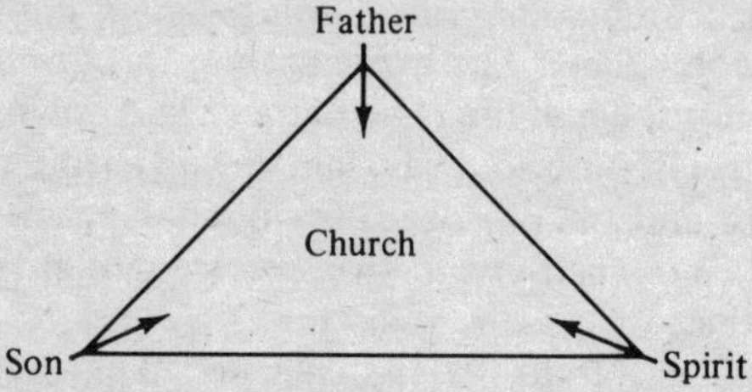

The Trinitarian Life is manifested on earth through the community of love in one mind and heart.

service they gave to be a response of love, and part of its life-giving mystery. Nevertheless, on the level of the service that we should perform, it is our great privilege to be Jesus' servants (Luke 17:10), just as the great men of old were called the servants of God (Exodus 4:10; Amos 3:7, etc), but from the viewpoint of intimacy with God we are His beloved, His friends, just as Moses was not merely a servant but also a personal friend of God (Exodus 33:11; Romans 8:33, etc).

The World's Hatred (15:18–16:4)

We are in such a divine atmosphere with Jesus revealing the new world order, where men and women trust God and each other, and serve one another in selfless love, that we have almost forgotten "those outside" who hate, kill and destroy, that world of power politics where the rich oppress the poor, and the few manipulate and control the many. With a jolt Jesus reminds us that our commission is to live out the new order of love in the midst of the old order of unbelief, hatred and fear, like leaven in the dough (Matthew 13:33). This challenge pulls us up short, making us realize why Jesus said that the branch would die if it did not feed off the vine. Without the power of God this command is impossible.

The disciples have witnessed the hatred levelled at Jesus, both during the ministry and especially during His passion and death. It is no consolation to know that they also are the inheritors of this hatred! Jesus offers them the full "package deal" of a Beloved Son, including the conflict between light and darkness which will continue through them. The world hates those who refuse to manipulate or be manipulated, those who cannot be "bought", those who operate on higher principles than their own power games. The world loves its own, whom it can "handle": it cannot handle love that lays down its life in selflessness. The powerful love of God and each other that exists within the Body of Believers serves to strengthen them as they go forth to face the onslaught of the world's hatred and opposition. What controls the world outside is power, what "controls" or motivates the Body is Love, that re-creative love of God transforming everyone and everything it touches.

Godly Love shows up worldly power and hate for what it is, so the disciples can expect persecution as their "normal" lot because the world loves its sin and the darkness which hides it (3:19–21). Jesus said that they would be expelled from the synagogues, and that the time would come "*when anyone who kills you will think he is doing a holy service to God*". The word John uses for this "service" to God means "to worship", so the persecutions were to be expected from very religious people, who would genuinely think that they were expressing their true worship to God by killing the Christians, as the Acts of the Apostles says of Paul before his conversion. It was his zeal for the Law that made him persecute and kill the followers of Jesus (Acts 22:1–5). By the time the gospel was written the Church had experienced several persecutions, both from Rome as well as from the Jewish Synagogue, and expulsions from the synagogues were accomplished facts rather than threats (see 1 John 3:13).

It would be a comfort to the early Christians to know that Jesus had forewarned them, as they would have expected Messianic bliss to follow the resurrection, from their reading of the Old Testament. It is interesting that Jesus says that the "true worship" would not be given to God by the persecutors but by the martyrs who laid down their lives in love. This is "messianic bliss" upside down, as Jesus tends to topple most of our conclusions.

As bearers of the Word of God, in the long line of the prophets, they will learn the pain of the prophet in the rejected word (Ezekiel 3:7; Isaiah 6:9–10; Jeremiah 1:19). As disciples they will be received in the same way as Jesus was, so they can expect to experience opposition to their teaching and claims as He did. But beloved disciples must realize that it is Jesus, the One who bears the Divine Name, that the world is persecuting in them, for they are His

Body, and the conflict with evil will continue to the end, the end of time and the end of evil. The blindness of the world is culpable and deliberate, for it is a rejection of the light and love of God, coming to them, both from Jesus incarnate before the resurrection, and Jesus present in the Body of Believers afterwards (see 1 John 4:5–6). The hatred of believers is hatred of the Father, who is the source of all this saving love. They have hated Jesus and the Father without cause, for the coming of Jesus was in answer to the prayer of Israel for the Messiah, and in Jesus God fulfilled all that He promised in the Messiah and much more, because the work continues through His beloved disciples until the end of time.

Chapter 16
Fruitful Vine in a Hostile Environment

The Spirit's Witness (16:5–15)

Just as Israel was on trial during the ministry, as Jesus witnessed to the Father, showing up her attachment to sin and darkness, and her refusal to receive all that God had offered her, even so the world will be on trial during the ministry of the beloved disciples, who will carry on the same witness for the same reason. However, Israel also put Jesus on trial, rejecting all His claims, refuting His teaching, and finally condemning Him to a shameful death in scorn and derision. In the same way the world will reject the teaching of the Church and persecute its members, killing thousands of them in every generation. In this mutual trial the Holy Spirit will play a major role of witnessing to Jesus and His teaching in and through the disciples. He will be their defence lawyer speaking up for the truth, one residing within them, whom the world cannot see or appreciate.

The disciples had been troubled at the thought of Jesus' impending departure (14:1), now they are sad at heart as they hear what is in store for them after He is gone. Their sadness is so great that they no longer ask Him where He is going. Jesus tells them that they cannot receive the gift of the Spirit unless He himself goes away, fully, selflessly in death, for He is the one to send the Spirit upon them as His special Messianic gift.

The Spirit's role in this world-trial will be to demonstrate that the world has no case against Jesus, as its spokesman, Pilate, will admit (19:5). The Spirit will show the world it was wrong about Jesus on three counts: sin, justice and judgement. The unbelievers among the Jews could not convict Jesus of sin (8:46) and neither can the world. It was they who sinned by refusing to accept God's divinely appointed envoy, who not only descended from the Father but also ascended after His ignominious death.

The sin of unbelief underlies all other sins, and, as we have heard in the last chapter, this unbelief is wilful and deliberate, so it is the world who sins, not Jesus. It is the painful privilege of the Body of Christ in every generation to convict the world of its sin by allowing the Holy Spirit to enlighten them regarding it first, and then by proclaiming it under the influence of the same Spirit. The disciples' sadness is understandable now that they realize that if they do the work they are called to, they will have an abrasive relationship with the world they serve. The unbelief of the world will not result in indifference but hostility.

Only the Holy Spirit can enlighten anyone regarding the REAL meaning of Jesus' death, and with the aid of this light we see the Beloved Son laying down His life for the very people who reject Him, His perfect love and humility showing up their hatred and unbelief. Thus the REAL guilt is demonstrated to those who want to know. His death, resurrection and ascension prove His claim that he came from the Father and returned to the Father. In fact, the very presence of the Paraclete is proof that Jesus is with the Father in glory, as it was only FROM THERE that He could send the Spirit. Therefore Jesus is proved just and righteous before the world, and the world in turn proved unjust and unrighteous.

The world that judged Jesus worthy of death was acting under the influence of "the Prince of this world", that principle of darkness which thought it could overcome the light, but it was Satan who was overcome in that glorious moment of the resurrection, when Light issued forth from a tomb of black darkness, and Life came forth from death, when against all the odds the tomb was transformed into a womb, losing its sting. The resurrection is God's definitive judgement on the world and Satan, because in God's court of justice, Jesus was judged worthy of eternal life, and He is present to His disciples through His Spirit.

So the Paraclete's presence with the disciples proves Jesus' claims. All the disciples have to do is "remain" in Jesus in mutual abiding, and the devil will be conquered for them personally, and the Kingdom of God will also advance. When Christians stay in union with Jesus, Satan has as much power to destroy them as he had with Jesus: they have conquered him.

Leaving the Paraclete with the new community, Jesus does not have to worry about teaching them everything NOW, for the Holy Spirit will reveal things as the need arises in the future. He will defend them against every enemy, both within and without themselves, for He will be with them throughout the entire mission of the Church. For each generation the Paraclete will interpret the teaching of Jesus, so that it will always be fresh bread that the Body is fed with, not the stale bread of yesteryear or the saints of old, but today's bread for today's saints. His duty is to lead both the individual as well as the community into the complete truth, about themselves, about Jesus, about the Father and about the world. They must continue their life-giving mission to the world.

The Holy Spirit will reveal things yet to come and "*He will glorify Me, since all He reveals to you will be taken from what is Mine. Everything the Father has is Mine* . . ." We see the interdependence of the Father, Son and Spirit as the source of revelation for the believing community. All that the Paraclete has comes from Jesus, all Jesus has comes from the Father, the ultimate source of all truth and life. The Paraclete's role is that of teacher and enlightener. He is the one to guide them along the way of truth and life, as was said of Wisdom in the Old Testament (Wisdom 9:11, 10:10; John 14:6).

The best preparation for the future, then, is a deep knowledge and understanding of Jesus and His teaching now, and the openness to let the Paraclete guide us daily along the way of truth. Thus the role of the Paraclete is to glorify Jesus, just as Jesus glorified the Father by revealing His word and doing His works. The Paraclete will do this in and through the beloved disciples.

Sadness into Gladness (16:16–33)

Jesus' early return is spoken of once more in that enigmatic way that warns us to read it on the level of "above" if understanding is to be with us. Soon the disciples will no longer see Jesus with the eyes of flesh, but then they will perceive Him with the inner eye of the spirit. The REAL seeing is the second one, not the first, as the world would contend! REAL seeing is on the level of the spirit, where REAL hearing and understanding lie also. The new vision that Jesus will give them in the New Age will enable them to walk with God with the ease of earthly friends walking together. They will "see" and be seen, know and be known, love and be loved. This will be the sorrow turned inside out, and the grief turned upside down. At the moment they are just confused by it all, because, before the spiritual vision is granted, a person cannot imagine what it is (1 Corinthians 2:10–16).

The coming death of their beloved Master will plunge them into personal grief, but there will also be the sorrow of witnessing the world's cruel joy as its gloats over its "victory" in destroying Jesus and "proving" Him wrong. But their sorrow will be both short-lived and life-giving, whereas the world's joy will be short-lived, and will be proved to have been totally wrong about Jesus anyway.

The ensuing joy of the disciples will be lasting, indeed everlasting, for their Master will rise, the first-born from the dead (Revelation 1:5), the New Man born to the life of the resurrection and everlasting joy (Acts 2:34–36).

The image of the woman in childbirth is a typical image depicting the birth pangs that Israel will have to endure before the day of the Messiah comes. In Isaiah 26:16–19 the people of Israel lamented that having suffered like a woman in childbirth they had only given birth to the wind . . . "*We have not given salvation to the earth, no inhabitants for the world have been brought to birth. Your dead will come back to life, your corpses will rise again. Wake up and sing you dwellers in the dust* . . . (Isaiah 66:7–10; Hosea 13:13–14; Revelation 12). The old Israel did not succeed in bringing forth salvation upon the earth, because in spite of all their privileges they were from "below". Only the one who was from "above" would succeed, AND bring their dead back to life, becoming the cause of everyone's joy, like a new Isaac. The disciples are the New Israel in formation, who will go through the terrible birth-pangs of the crucifixion with Jesus, to bring forth the New Man to the life of the resurrection, and He will be immediately snatched up to heaven (Revelation 12: 1–5).

John speaks of the *great suffering*, sharp, intense suffering, that Jesus will have to endure in the passion. The affliction of the disciples will begin then, and continue throughout the persecutions to come, until the final birth pangs that will precede the Parousia (Daniel 12:1; Zephaniah 1:14–15; Mark 13:19, 24). This great affliction is followed by great joy, the joy of victory and glory for Jesus; the joy of seeing Jesus in the resurrection appearances, for the disciples initially, but more permanently the joy of permanent mutual abiding in love for the whole of their personal lives, as well as that of the community of faith. Then there is the everlasting bliss to follow the Final Glorious Coming of Jesus.

With this resurrection joy will come the mutual love and friendship with the Father and the Son, a union so deep that the Father will relate to them, and love them with the same love with which He loves Jesus. The Father, Son and Disciples will be so completely one that Jesus will not have to intercede for them, their requests ARE His. "*When that day comes you will ask in my name; and I do not say that I shall pray to the Father for you, because the Father Himself loves you for loving Me . . .*" Besides, He will pray with them, for them and through them. At its deepest point their prayer will be Jesus praying to the Father IN THEM through the Paraclete.

This prayer can claim all that is needed for the redemption of one individual, and also the cosmos in the same breath. The Father sees His Son in the disciples. Since Jesus dwells in the disciples their petitions are in His name, and since Jesus is one with the Father, all petitions are granted in His name too. They have not asked in His name up to now, because full union with Him is only possible AFTER the resurrection and glory of Jesus (Ephesians 2:18). It is, too, only then that the disciples will be able to hear Jesus speak clearly, not as they do now in the enigmatic language of one from "above". They themselves will be born from above then, so hearing and seeing on that level will be open to them. Their joy will be total and complete as they walk with opened eyes in union with Father, Son and Spirit.

Before all that the very painful scattering of the disciples must happen, when the shepherd will be struck as scripture said He would. The night must come before the dawn of the New Age, and the night will plunge each one of them into the darkness of their own being to see what is there, so that with the dawn of the New Age, they will let it all go to the Lord and be transformed into the new "stuff" of eternal life. When they have scattered and left Him alone physically, He will have the Father with Him spiritually, so he will not be alone in the REAL sense.

The victory over the world that He is going to achieve must be repeated in every person, that of the transformation of that person into Christ, so that Love will dominate and reign in that life. There can be nothing but pain and sorrow in a world dominated by power and the egocentric principle, that enslaves both itself and others. It is the privilege of the believing community to help transform the world into a place that is born from "above" where Love has won the victory. "*I have told you all this so that you may find peace in Me. In the world you will have hardship, but be courageous: I have conquered the world.*"

Chapter 17

The Prayer of a Beloved Son

With the ministry and the Last Discourse over, all that remains is for the Beloved Son to pray the new Body into reality, which He will do now, and then pay the price for its birth, which He will do in the next two chapters. This concludes the earthly side and initiates the heavenly side of Jesus' work, which coincides with the beginning of the earthly ministry of the beloved disciples. Jesus' Passover is an "ending" which is a beginning, a thought we now come to expect from John. If we have been in the warm atmosphere of the Last Supper with Jesus and His disciples for some time, we now enter the Holy of Holies as we listen in to the intimate conversation between Father and Son. There is a sense of awe and wonder too, as we realize that we have been invited, not only to listen in, but to enter into communion with Them for the whole of our lives. As we had begun to realize in the Last Discourse, heaven is not only over our heads, it is also under our feet. We are invited to live this heavenly life on earth as our daily reality (Colossians 3:1–4).

The farewell speeches of the great men of old often ended with prayer for the protection of their descendants, and for their teaching to be lived out in them – for example, Moses in Deuteronomy 33. Jesus does that now, in the prayer that has been called "the priestly prayer of Christ", and also John's version of what we call the "Our Father". In Deuteronomy 33 Moses turns to the heavens to pray for his followers and also turns to the followers to bless them. Here we find Jesus turning to His Father in heaven in matters that concern the future of His beloved disciples. He is called Priest because He stands before God making intercession for us (Romans 8:34; Letter to Hebrews 7:25). The whole tone of this lovely prayer indicates that for John, Jesus is already "on the other side" speaking in the hearing hearts of His beloved disciples. Eternity has already broken in on time, and Jesus speaks now as things will be then: "*I am no longer in the world*", He says. In this prayer Jesus really ascends to the Father: it is really THE prayer of His Hour.

This prayer parallels the "Our Father" of the Synoptic gospels (Matthew 6:9–13; Luke 11:2–4) in that Jesus addresses Himself to the "Father" in heaven (17:1, 5, 11, 21, 24, 25). His request for God to be "hallowed" is the same as "glorified" here. Its overall concern is with God's Kingdom in the completion of the work that the Father gave the Son, which will continue through the disciples. The request "may your will be done" in the "Our Father" refers to this work also, and both are concerned with the protection of the disciples from the Evil One. Yet John's version is unique in that it is not just instruction on how to pray as a beloved family member. It is instead an invasion of the privacy of the Father and Son in communion with each other.

The confidence of the Son is such that what He asks is granted because of the union of wills existing between Them. The prayer is unique in its "otherness", in the total absence of anything to do with "I". It has all to do with "You" and "them", and the "them" is so comprehensive that it covers not only the disciples who are alive before the passion, and at the time of writing the gospels, but every person of every generation who reads these wonderful words. At that moment we, too, enter with Jesus into the very presence of God, and know that we are loved and interceded for, that OUR heaven is requested and granted by One who loved us to the laying down of His life, not only that HE could pick it up again, but that we, too, could pick it up and live at the highest level of our being.

This prayer of Jesus is public in so far as the disciples were allowed to listen in to it. Like the time He prayed at the tomb of Lazarus, it was for their sakes: He did not need to verbalize His prayer, which could be summarized totally in that extraordinary word "ABBA", which releases God's Creative Fathering upon the needy world. One need only acknowledge it to release its wonder upon the cosmos. Because this prayer has an audience it also contains instruction for the disciples, that the Church would continue this intercessory role for the world when Jesus had departed from them. The Holy Spirit residing in them will enable them to pray like this, as was Jesus' wish (Matthew 6:9).

Glorious Love (17:1–8)

The whole prayer is based on this one word "Abba", which is what every small child calls their own Daddy, and it contains all the possessiveness of love and intimacy that the child experiences on its Daddy's knee. As the gospel proceeded, the name "Father" grew upon us into the maturity of "Father and Son", while keeping the child-like quality of humility, love and openness. Abba keeps before us the complete dependence of the Son on the Father, yet as we saw, the Father conferred upon the Son authority over all flesh (17:2). The title Abba, then, involves mutual knowledge, understanding of the heart, and intimacy in relationship which is expressed in trust and union of wills.

For the Son to say "Abba" releases the Father to say "Son", with the affirmation that that entails, which the Synoptics give at Jesus' Baptism, and at the Transfiguration (Luke 3:22, 9:35, etc), and John gave in the several affirmations regarding the Father loving the Son (3:35, 5:20, 10:7). The prayer Abba elicits from the Father the revelation "I AM FATHER": the origin of all life, light, goodness, love. I father You, share My life with You, and through You give it to others . . . I authored the whole redemptive process whereby everyone can be released from slavery to sin and darkness, and freed from the realm of "below", where they labour under the infernal influence of the prince of this world. So when the Son, in prayer, releases Abba to declare "I AM FATHER" He releases the divine realm upon the world, with all its beauty and glory. To say "Abba", then, is to say everything that is necessary.

The mutual love of Father and Son leads them to glorify each other. The "glory" involves a visible manifestation of Their majesty by acts of power. The particular act of power Jesus requests is that He be allowed to give eternal life to all believers, a fact that would prove His being "with" the Father, and not, as His enemies will claim, a defeated criminal. All that Jesus has promised in this gospel in terms of life, light, bread, living water, etc, can only be given after His death, so the Father's glory is tied up with the Son's. The acceptance of this request by the Father will redound to His own glory and to the salvation of believers, hence it is not "my" glory in the wrong sense. Throughout the ministry John kept reminding us that the signs revealed Jesus' glory, but that was only by way of SIGN, now He wants to confer the REALITY signified by all His acts of power (1:14, 2:11, 11:4, 40, 12:28).

When Jesus lays down His life in that ultimate act of love, it will reveal the reality of I AM upon an amazed world, the "I AM" reality of both Father and Son, and their mutual love for all. The Son's part is to glorify the Father by His perfect humility and surrender to His will, while giving His life for sinners who do not deserve such love and compassion. The Father's side is to raise His Son from the dead, put Him at His right hand in glory, and because – "*you have given him power over all humanity* . . . " the Son will use this power to give eternal life to . . . "*all those you have entrusted to Him*". Father and Son worked in tandem during Jesus' ministry, and this reality continues after His death, to show that Their relationship was not just communion of love but union of action.

With that authority He has been given over all humanity Jesus wants to confer a most precious gift, that of "knowing" God. This word has a very special meaning in biblical usage. It implies a deep personal "heart" knowledge such as two lovers have of each other, or faithful partners in marriage. It is not intellectual knowledge gleaned from books, but knowledge gained from personal relationship. It implies a committed relationship that will bear fruit, in this case the fruit of the Spirit (which we discussed in the previous chapter). Jesus knows that His community will die if it ever reduces itself to merely book knowledge of God, a dead theology, instead of a constantly lived reality. His disciples are to "know" the Father AND Jesus in this special way, so that their proclamation of His message will bear the marks of true witnesses. This intimate knowledge of God was promised in the prophets, and Jesus seeks to fulfil it (Jeremiah 24:7, 31:31–34; Habakkuk 2:14).

Jesus is about to depart from the world having finished the work that the Father gave Him to do. This special work was to reveal the divine name, I AM, to the disciples, who are the Father's gift to the Son, the "bride" who is being prepared for her Bridegroom in the marriage of heaven and earth that will take place in the Paschal mystery (3:29). Jesus, the Bridegroom, is the bearer of the divine name, and the bride, if she is to participate in this mystery, must know this reality. She must know that the Person of the Father was revealed in and through the Son, that His Word and His works revealed the I AM to them: that, in Jesus, they have access to God Himself.

When God revealed Himself to Moses He said: I AM (EGO EIMI). It was THIS reality that Jesus revealed to the disciples, who would only understand it fully when Jesus had been lifted up fully (8:28). Isaiah 52:6 had promised that when the messianic times dawned the people would know the divine name (Ego Eimi) as Moses had known it. Jesus wants His missionaries to go to all the world bearing this revelation, that in Jesus EGO EIMI was revealed. It is this knowledge that makes the disciples realize at long last that Jesus DID, in fact, come from God and return to Him. Now they realize too that the teaching they pass on to others comes from the same source, so they can teach with authority. They know for certain that Jesus was the "One sent by God" whose words they must listen to and obey (Deuteronomy 18:18).

Prayer for Disciples (9–19)

The disciples are an essential part of Jesus' mission, so He intercedes for them now, asking for what the Father most wants to give them. For the moment He is not concerned with the cosmos "out there", for the disciples will deal with that in their mission. It is more important just now to deal with the training and protection of the people who will carry on this mission in His name. They have to live the reality of I AM in the midst of the unbelief of the world, so Jesus requests their protection from the contamination of that unbelief which would destroy their testimony.

"*Keep those You have given Me true to Your name, so that they may be one like Us.*" If the Father does not protect the little community, it cannot maintain its oneness with Them or with each other, and so will lose its credibility before the world. Another reason for protection is the fact that they will be plunged into spiritual warfare as soon as the mission begins (17:15; 1 John 2:15–17). Not only are they to remain true to what they have been taught, but the divine name itself will be a protection to them. Proverbs 18:10 says that the name of the Lord is a strong tower; those who are upright run to it and find safety. All future disciples will find that I AM is their sure haven at all times, and their security in danger (18:5–8). Thus there is no need for any disciple to be lost spiritually or eternally, unless they so choose by their free decision. Jesus, the incarnate I AM, had watched over His disciples carefully, and His protection ensured that none were lost except poor Judas, who chose to go in spite of all the gestures of love on the part of his Master.

Their knowledge of I AM and their living of love in community with the indwelling of Father and Son in the Spirit will ensure their complete joy amidst the darkness and unbelief of the world. This interior joy is independent of all external circumstances and will be their strong tower in the days ahead, for the "joy of the Lord will be their strength", as Nehemiah 8:10 declared. The Synoptic gospels also testify to the power of this interior joy to overcome even persecution and martyrdom (Matthew 5:11), and 1 Thessalonians 1:6 shows that it became reality among the early Christians, who knew from their personal experience that Jesus had kept His promise to them.

The sent one now becomes the sender, as Jesus officially announces that the disciples are being sent into the world as He was sent: "*As you sent Me into the world, I have sent them into the world.*" Jesus was sent into the world as the bearer of the divine name, and the bearer of the Word. The disciples are now being sent with authority to reveal both in Jesus' name. For this they must be consecrated, set apart for this awesome responsibility, and somehow they must become holy, even as the Father and Jesus are holy (Leviticus 19:2).

In the Old Testament priests and prophets were consecrated for mission, and this holds true for the disciples (see Exodus 28:41). They must be anointed with the Word if they are to preach it effectively, so their consecration is in "the truth" (17:6,14). The indwelling Spirit of Truth is there to help them (14:17, 16:13), and since the Spirit is the

Holy Spirit, holiness is expected of them also (2 Thessalonians 2:13). This was because they were to join the long line of the prophets who were the bearers of God's Word. They had to be prepared and consecrated for this exalted office (see Jeremiah 1:5). To bring this about Jesus consecrates Himself as a sacrificial victim in His final Passover. It is His life-giving death that imparts consecration to His disciples. In his final "lifting up" in the Ascension, the mantle of His prophetic office will fall upon them, and the descent of the spirit at Pentecost will give the empowering from on high that is needed for their mission (Acts 1:9–11, 2:1–4).

Prayer for Unity (17:20–26)

Now Jesus turns His attention to the distant future, foreseeing the success of the mission of the Church. He wants all believers to participate in the communion of Father and Son. Thus witness is given to the unbelieving world, not only of a Son in total surrender of union, love and obedience to the Father, but also of everyone who calls themselves disciples. "*May they all be one, just as, Father, You are in Me and I am in You, so that they also may be one in Us, so that the world may believe it was You who sent Me.*"

We know from chapter sixteen that this does not mean that the cosmos will ACCEPT this testimony, but Jesus wants it to continue down the ages anyway. Thus the world will continue to see ordinary people live both in union with God and with each other. The source of this union is the Trinity of Love, which is a diversity in unity, and unity in diversity, and this is to be reflected among believers. This unity is God's work and cannot be achieved by merely human means. Besides, the community of beloved disciples participate in Jesus' glory as they manifest His presence and power among them through acts of power as they continue His ministry on earth.

The union between Jesus and believers is not just internal and private, it is externalized through fraternal love and service, and therefore is very concrete in its expression and in its fruits. If the world's eyes were opened it would see wonderingly that the loving service of the Christian community has its source in God, that it is a reflection of divine love. In fact, it IS divine love because God is its source and power and motivation. God's infinite Love which was mediated first through Jesus is now mediated through the Christian community.

The finale to this magnificent prayer, which is also a revelation of the heart of Jesus, is a request that the beloved disciples would find their eternal destiny "with" Jesus in the presence of the Father. Thus having been lifted up into the realm of "above" through being born of the Spirit; having lived on this level through mutual indwelling of love and unity, they are finally brought to their heavenly home. "*I want those You have given Me to be with Me where I am, so that they may always see My glory . . .* " The privileges of mutual indwelling in love are everlasting, but the disciples will see the definitive glory of Jesus as the Beloved Son when they see Him in the bosom of the Father whence He came.

As He leaves to depart for the Father's home, Jesus addresses Him again in that loving childlike way with which he began the prayer: "Abba". Earlier He called Him "*Holy Father*", now He calls Him the "Upright One" or the "Just One", as the Father will manifest both His Holiness and His Justice in the events of the Hour of Jesus. In fact, He alone is holy and just in the real sense. The unbelieving cosmos will never see this until the final judgement because their unbelief blinds them to the truth. The holiness and rightness of all that the Father and Son do will be seen by the beloved disciples, because Jesus has revealed the Divine Name to them, and now they KNOW God. He will continue to reveal the Father through the future mission of the believing community.

Just as the Father had revealed Himself on Sinai and then came to live among His people in the Tabernacle in the desert, just so has Jesus embodied the presence and glory of God throughout His lifetime which was spent revealing the Father to the disciples. Now as He leaves them in death He will take up residence in the hearts of His disciples as in a Tabernacle, thus He will always "*be in them*" (Exodus 24:16, 40:34; John 1:14, 20:28).

Chapter 18

Beloved Son on Trial

Coming from the serenity of the communion of Father and Son in the last chapter, we are suddenly plunged again, with shock, into the world of darkness and unbelief. From the quiet warm conversations Jesus has had with His beloved disciples and His Father, we are thrown into the frenzy of activity from Jesus' enemies, who are suddenly in a rush to kill Him before Passover, the following day. The tempo is speeded up, so that several "trials" plus an execution take place in so short a time that one feels breathless just reading it.

The shock effect on the disciples must have been enormous, coming as they did from the security of the Last Supper, where Jesus was calm and everything was under control. For us, too, there is shock, as we have probably forgotten that Judas went out into the night to join Jesus' enemies (13:32). Perhaps without adverting to it, we have been in the realm of "above", enjoying the joy and peace of the Kingdom of God, and now the realm of "below" is thrown upon us and we see it clearly, maybe for the first time.

As we enter this awful realm of darkness we are faced with the struggle for power and control that rules here. On the one hand we have Caiaphas and the Sanhedrin desperately holding on to their institutions, their Jewish faith and their national heritage, and in the process prepared to kill an innocent man in the name of God. On the other hand, Pilate and the Roman Empire, as desperately trying to subdue this rebellious province, ready to kill and compromise for political advantage. History has proved that these two powers, representing the unbelieving cosmos, were willing mutually to manipulate and eventually destroy each other. An innocent prisoner stands between them to pay the price for their hatred and fear.

John approaches the passion in his own unique fashion, using the traditional material at his disposal in a dramatic way that underscores the theological meaning of the events being shown. To understand him we will have to view the passion from the theological position of the gospel as a whole, and go into it knowing who Jesus is. Then we will see that John wants us to "read" each event from several angles so that its shock effect can register. Not only will we have to view the events from "above" in order to understand them, but John also uses a dramatic stage technique to illustrate his point. This can be seen, for example, where Peter's denial is run front stage to the interrogation of Jesus before Annas and Caiaphas. The trial before Pilate has three stage positions, with Pilate and the Jews front stage, Pilate and Jesus alone back stage, and on centre stage Jesus and the soldiers who mock Him as king of the Jews.

Then, typical of John, we have to remember that the judge is not Pilate, who in his ignorance passes judgement on the judge of the whole world, but Jesus, who passes judgement on both Pilate and Caiaphas, declaring Pilate the less guilty of the two. The reader also knows whence Jesus' Kingdom comes, and that the embodiment of the truth stands before Pilate's unseeing eyes. When Pilate declares, "Here is the man", we know that the full revelation of who Jesus is would have terrified the man, Pilate, who, in his darkness, would not be able to stand before the Beloved Son, the Light of the World. Caiaphas is continually called the High Priest in the account, yet the reader is aware that Jesus is the true and only High Priest of the New Covenant. Finally, when the soldiers mock Jesus as the king of the Jews they merely intend to insult the Jews, yet the reality is that Jesus IS the king of the Jews, though unrecognized by either Jew or Gentile.

From this we see that John is proclaiming that Jesus is the true Messianic King of the Jews, the true High Priest of the new religion, the true judge, the true Temple, and the Lamb of God who takes away the sin of the world at the final Passover, in which He fulfilled all that had been prophesied. We are also being told that though the powers of darkness appear to be in control, in fact it is Jesus who is. They can only touch Him when He deliberately surrenders to them, and He does this out of perfect love for His Father and for His disciples, "His own". John shows that both Jews and Gentiles were used by the forces of darkness in trying to eliminate the Son of God. So if we read the account with the opened eyes of one born from above we will indeed see through these awful events to the Hour of Glory of the Son of Man.

The Arrest of Jesus (18:1–11)

After the supper Jesus and His disciples went out into the night to face the powers of darkness that were stalking the land looking for Him. They crossed the Kidron valley to a garden on the Mount of Olives (Luke 22:39), where Jesus often met with his disciples to pray. At this point the Synoptics mention the agony of Jesus, but John omits it to retain the dignity of Jesus and to demonstrate His complete control of all that happened. Judas' treason consisted of informing the authorities of this place where Jesus could be arrested at night without the danger of riots from His supporters.

Suddenly the garden was invaded by a large group of Roman soldiers with a detachment of Temple police headed by Judas, who would be the only one to recognize Jesus in these circumstances. However, John points out that the fact that they come armed *with lanterns and torches and weapons* to meet the Light of the World shows that they are the agents of darkness, and that they are totally blind to the truth. This is indeed THE NIGHT that Jesus spoke about, where people who walked in it would stumble (11:10, 12:35) because they had no light to guide them. Interior light is what is missing in those who arrest Jesus. But there will come a moment of complete victory for the Beloved Son when His Kingdom will be fully established, then no one will need any artificial light, for the Lord God will be the only light that they need (Revelation 22:5).

Jesus came forward to confront the forces of darkness, asking them the vital question: "*Who are you looking for?*" When this question was asked of the disciples in 1:38 they were looking for the Messiah and for life. It will be asked of Mary of Magdala after the resurrection (20:15), and she too will be looking for Jesus her Saviour and for life. These men are looking for Jesus of Nazareth only to put Him to death. So we see that in their response to Jesus the secret thoughts of many hearts are revealed. The light continues to show up what is there in its X-ray effect.

John shows clearly that Jesus is in control, and that the police cannot arrest Him until He surrenders to them. This He does not do until He reveals clearly who He is, and then they must take responsibility for their actions afterwards. In response Jesus replied: EGO EIMI. Once again He gave them the divine name, and they fell back before His majesty. John is showing the fulfilment of several prophecies here, as falling prostrate before the majesty of God was the normal response given in the Old Testament. At the same time the prophecy of Psalm 27:2, which says that "*When the wicked advance against me to eat me up, they, my opponents, my enemies, are the ones to stumble and fall*" was fulfilled (Psalm 56:9; Isaiah 11:4; Daniel 2:46; Revelation 1:17). Jesus will not surrender until the disciples can escape from their clutches, as He had promised that the divine name would be their protection. He does not call on its protection for Himself but for those whom He loved (17:12).

Peter, though obviously motivated by love for Jesus, but whose thinking is still on the level of "below", made a futile effort to prevent Jesus' death. We know from Luke's gospel (22:38) that the disciples were carrying two swords. He is still of the mind to fight FOR Jesus instead of allowing Jesus to fight for his salvation just now. Jesus again reminds him that the sword is the weapon of "the world" while His surrender to His Father is the "weapon" of the realm of "above". If Jesus does not drink the cup of suffering there will be no cup of joy in the gift of salvation (Psalm 23:5). Peter must, eventually, come to understand that this cup is the Father's gift to Jesus, before it can become Jesus' gift to His disciples.

Interrogation of Jesus (18:12–27)

The binding of Jesus, when He surrenders into the hands of sinners, is a very dramatic event. He came down from "above" to unbind us from the slavery to sin and death, and to free us to walk a new life, yet we, sinners, bound Him and killed Him, caught up as we were in the realm of darkness. He, alone, can "unbind" sin and death. He will be bound again, in grave cloths, when He surrenders to death, but the unbinding of the Beloved Son will be the most dramatic moment of all, when He surrenders Himself into the life of glory. We were introduced to this theme in the unbinding of Lazarus, a theme of setting free a person into new life. It is the fulfilment of the binding of Isaac by his father, Abraham, when he went to sacrifice his son for love of God. But when God gave Isaac back to his father the unbinding of the boy became a symbol of resurrection, since the boy was given back from the "dead" to his father (Genesis 22; Letter to Hebrews 11:17–19). John makes sure that we understand that Jesus was captured and executed both by the Roman authorities as well as by the Jewish, hence responsibility for the death of Jesus will lie on Jew and Gentile alike.

The prisoner was taken for interrogation before the High Priest first. The House of Annas, which produced four High Priests, and Caiaphas, a son-in-law, was in firm control of Jewish affairs. They were noted for their greed, wealth and power. Annas, the former High Priest (A.D. 6–16), still wielded a lot of power, and so Jesus was taken to him first. It was Caiaphas who had prophesied that Jesus should die for the people.

Two significant disciples were present to witness this interrogation, the beloved disciple and Peter, the two who would also be the first male witnesses to the tomb of Jesus. The beloved disciple was known to the High Priest (some, presuming that this person is John the son of Zebedee, claim that his father, who was in the salt fish trade, supplied fish to the High Priest's house. Others claim that he may have been related to the High Priest's family, but neither theory can be proved) and so was able to go into the courtroom, but Peter stayed outside within hearing distance. Peter's love for Jesus is well attested in the gospels. Now that his Master is in need he follows in order to be with Him, while all the other disciples flee in fear, but unfortunately he is not able to be "with" Jesus in the right sense yet, as he still belongs to the world of "below" and his denial will prove it.

Backstage Jesus is questioned about His disciples and His teaching, but remains firm and loyal, denying nothing of who or what He is. Peter, on the other hand, is questioned by a servant girl frontstage and denies everything, denies that he knew Jesus or had anything to do with Him. To become a beloved disciple Peter will need to go through the death of self to pass over to the real life from "above" where he can join Jesus in His witness and love. His testimony right now is the exact opposite of Jesus. When asked if he is a disciple he declares, in the hearing of everyone, including Jesus: "I AM NOT", whereas Jesus declared before His captors: "I AM." Before the death and resurrection of Jesus, not only is Peter's true witness I AM NOT, but so was John the Baptist's and indeed so is that of everyone before Redemption. Only after Jesus has been "lifted up" will it be possible for each one of us to become a beloved son and pick up our true selves in the glory of "I AM".

Backstage the interrogators abuse Jesus by breaking the law in making Him answer questions when the law demanded that the prisoner keep silent in case he condemn himself. Only the witnesses should speak. That the High Priests would blatantly break the law like this showed just how unscrupulous they were, and how determined to kill Jesus. Jesus correctly said; "*Why ask Me*?" They should ask the properly accredited witnesses. Here He is reminding them that this is not a trial in any sense since there are no witnesses, no jury and no just judge. Jesus' words also echo those of the Lord in the Old Testament. Neither had spoken in secret, but for all the world to hear (Isaiah 45:19, 48:16). The result for Jesus was abuse, because an ordinary peasant from the country would be expected to cower before the might of the High Priest, but Jesus shows His equality and freedom. It is an interesting point that Jesus asked the man who struck Him to own his own violence. He did not turn the other cheek to accept needless abuse (see Luke 6:28–29), since the REAL "turning of the other cheek" was His surrender to the powers of darkness in order to let God's higher plan come into operation.

Trial before Pilate (18:28–40)

For John this is the real trial of Jesus of Nazareth, and he presents it in seven dramatic scenes in order to bring out the full theological content. The trial of Jesus before the Sanhedrin, spoken about in the Synoptic gospels, is omitted, because John dealt with its various aspects in chapters five to eleven. It is the trial before the world-power on which John concentrates. The world, too, must decide for or against the light, and this Pilate will do in its name. There will be two main stages in the drama, the calm quiet atmosphere of the meetings between Pilate and Jesus backstage, and the frenzied shouts of hate and cruelty frontstage in the Praetorium.

Pilate's constant crossing from one to the other emphasizes the struggle going on within him, for every time he finds himself alone with Jesus he can see at least the innocence of the prisoner, but confusion returns as he faces the political pressure of the Jewish leaders outside. Pilate's mistake is that he tries to play the game both ways. On the one hand he wants to set an innocent man free, and on the other he wants to give the "blood" the Jews demand. As the game proceeds it becomes more dangerous and both protagonists lose out. Pilate forces the Jews to deny all their messianic hopes and proclaim Caesar their king, while he is forced to do their bidding, thus losing all credibility as a leader. Between the two stands a prisoner who will die ANYWAY. This sinful game leads to the destruction of all who participate in it, yet it reveals the secret thoughts of all concerned, and the REAL struggle going on in the world.

Behind all this strife John proclaims the kingship of Jesus, which is the subject of the discussion between Pilate and Jesus. Pilate will eventually declare Jesus king before the Jews. Jesus will have a mock crowning and enthronement as king by the Roman soldiers, and when Jesus is presented to the Jewish nation as their king, they will disclaim Him and choose the secular power in the name of Caesar. Thus John illustrates the theme of Psalm 2 (Acts 4:25–26), that the kings of the earth (represented by Pilate) gathered together with the rulers of the people (the Sanhedrin) against the Lord and against His Anointed One.

Scene 1: Jesus is Accused (18:28–32)

This scene opens at daybreak. The dawning of this day is of vital importance to everyone, for it is the day of the Lord in a very real sense, even though the workers of darkness will be very busy, thinking that it is THEIR day. But as we have heard, the darkness will not succeed in overcoming the light (1:5). Unkown to them it is the day that the Lord has made, in which Christians would rejoice for evermore (Psalm 118:24). The leaders took Jesus from the house of Caiaphas to the Praetorium for trial by Pilate, the incarnation of Roman world power in Israel. If they were to eat Passover they were forbidden to enter the house of pagans, as it would involve incurring ritual defilement. These men, who did not baulk at premeditated murder, were, nevertheless, scrupulously correct about their observance of religious ritual. Their hypocrisy is obvious and serves to illustrate that religion without morality is monstrous.

They handed Jesus over officially then to the Roman authority, to try Him for a capital crime. Thus Jesus was doubly "handed over", first by His friend Judas, and now by His own people in the person of their leaders who hated Him without cause (15:25). Pilate will also hand Him over for crucifixion, so Jesus is betrayed by everyone, and for no other reason than their own sinfulness. Pilate demanded the charge, so the leaders changed the real charge of blasphemy (10:33; Matthew 26:65) to a civil charge that would hold good in a civil court. They accused Jesus of being a revolutionary, one who set Himself up in opposition to Caesar.

The Jewish punishment for blasphemy was stoning, and we saw several attempts to stone Jesus during the gospel. But the leaders wanted to disgrace Jesus in the eyes of the people to the point that His followers would drop His ideas altogether when they saw Him die on a cross, a punishment which only the Roman power could inflict. Ironically, in doing this, the leaders were party to Jesus' being "lifted up", on the cross first but then in glory, a thing they never intended! They wanted to prevent the people from believing in Him, but His lifting up will draw all people to Him, not just Jewish disciples (11:48, 12:32).

Scene 2: Jesus is King (18:33–38)

Alone with Jesus backstage Pilate questions the prisoner regarding His kingship. With his jails full of revolutionaries and subversives Pilate would recognize a criminal on sight, hence his amazed and perhaps cynical question: "*Are* You *the king of the Jews*?" Pilate is aware that the charge against Jesus is false (Mark 15:11), that it concerns some religious problem, yet he must investigate whether there is any political overtone to it (Luke 23:2). As soon as Jesus speaks we realize that this trial is upside down, and that the Roman Governor is on trial before the king of the Jews. Pilate is a man facing the light of God's truth and must decide for or against, like every other person who meets Jesus. Hence Jesus questions Pilate as to whether he is personally interested or whether he is JUST investigating a case before him. Pilate's cynical "Am I a Jew?" reveals his well-known hatred of Jesus' people, the very ones who have handed Him over to Pilate.

Pilate's demand to know what Jesus has done in order to bring Him to judgement is answered in the truly Johannine way, when Jesus reveals the true nature of His kingship. Jesus admits to being a king, but something Pilate could never understand is that this kingly rule of Jesus belongs to the realm of "above", as He does Himself and as do those who follow Him. Like Himself, His kingdom is IN the world but not OF it. It takes neither its power, its authority nor its influence from the world, and its members do not fight, as Peter had to be reminded at the arrest (18:10). It belongs to the realm of the Spirit and is concerned with truth, which is REALITY as it really is. Jesus is the unique revealer of the truth about God, about man and about the true reality of the world, and to be confronted by this truth is a demand to accept or reject it with dreadful consequences. Jesus knows that His rejection by the Jews is because He has given evidence against the world that its ways are evil (7:7). The "world", as represented by Pilate, must make its choice. There is no escape from this.

As far as politics is concerned, Pilate can now relax, for whatever Jesus is talking about, it does not conflict with Rome's political interests in Palestine. But Pilate is not on the side of truth, and will not listen to the voice of Jesus, the only and unique revealer of truth. As one of the "other sheep" (10:16) that Jesus is interested in taking into His sheepfold, Pilate is given an opportunity to hear the voice of the shepherd, be born again of the Spirit and join the Kingdom of God. But the moment of decision is lost as Pilate loses patience with all this talk of "religion" and other worldliness when he has a case to try and a city to keep quiet at Passover, the most dangerous time in Israel. Coming as he does from the pagan Roman Empire, with its multiplicity of gods and religions, he cynically asks: "Truth? What is that?", and walks away from his moment of salvation . . . one more rich man too involved in the affairs of this world to care about another world (Mark 10:25; Luke 1:53, 16:19, etc).

Scene 3: Barabbas or Jesus (18:38–40)

The consequences of Pilate's decision against the truth will fall upon Him sooner than he realizes. Leaving the inner stage he went out frontstage, and declared Jesus innocent of the charges made against Him. The Jews had brought Jesus before Pilate as a revolutionary, now Pilate reveals the sham by producing a REAL revolutionary, a man in jail for sedition and murder (Mark 15:7). He had the same name as Jesus, Barabbas, which means "son of the father". Ironically Pilate has given the Jews their REAL choice: they are to choose either Jesus the Beloved Son of the Father, or a sinful son of a sinful father, a REAL subversive.

Pilate forced the real motivation out of the Jews when they chose to have Barabbas released knowing that he was a bandit! Knowing that, why were they so anxious to kill Jesus if He, too, were a revolutionary? There is a cross-reference here to 10:1, 8, 9, 10, where the Good Shepherd is compared to robbers and bandits. He gives life while they break in to steal and destroy. "They" represent the forces of darkness in contrast to Jesus, the Light of the World. They reject their King-Messiah in favour of the realm of darkness and destruction. They have chosen a son of darkness over against Jesus, the Beloved Son of the Father, so caught up are they in winning their point against Pilate.

But the Jews are not the only losers in this dangerous game. By producing Barabbas, Pilate is forced by them to release someone against his better judgement, someone who is a REAL threat to Rome! When Pilate refuses to listen to the voice of Jesus he is compelled to listen to the voice of the Jews, and becomes eventually a pawn in a dangerous political game. Having rejected Jesus the revealer of truth, he proceeds to make false and unjust decisions one after the other, until finally he crucifies incarnate truth.

Chapter 19

Beloved Son "Lifted Up"

Scene 4: Coronation (19:1–3)

In the following scenes the political charge against Jesus quickly fades into the background and the real charge is brought to the fore. Despairing of winning Pilate over, the Jews resort to political blackmail that forces Pilate to act against his better judgement, when he discovers that they have the power to destroy him. Thus a new situation has developed: someone has to die; will it be Pilate or Jesus? Barabbas was quickly dealt with, but now Pilate's political career is in question. Thus cornered he resorts to action that incenses the Jews, as he proceeds to insult their claims to have a king. At the same time he makes a warped, but probably sincere, last attempt to release Jesus. His thinking appears to be that if the Jews want blood he will give it to them, by reducing Jesus to an inhuman sight through scourging.

Pilate ordered Jesus to be scourged, a punishment that went with a capital crime, a punishment so brutal that many a man died raving mad under it. It involved whipping with an instrument which had leather thongs into which pieces of lead were stuck, so that it ripped the flesh off the victim, who was scourged from head to foot, back and front, reducing him to a bloodied mess. Jesus not only remained conscious throughout this ordeal, but silent and majestic. Yet He had not even been sentenced!

Pilate's sense of justice is seen to be warped and untruthful, because he himself had declared Jesus innocent (18:39). If he intends to solicit pity for Him by presenting Him to the Jewish leaders after this, he will fail, for they see

Pilate reduced to a position of powerlessness where he has to bargain for Jesus' release, something the Jews have no intention of granting. Thus power has passed from Pilate to the Jewish leaders, something they would have capitalized on later.

Surprisingly, the Roman soldiers seemed free to violate Jesus as they pleased, with no interference from Pilate. After the scourging they made a human effigy of Him as a pretender-king. Dressing Him in a kingly robe, they crowned Him King of the Jews with a crown of thorns, which was a symbol of the curse of sin. This humble king is not only wearing the symbol of destruction from the realm of "below", but He is also a Lamb on His way to release everyone from this curse (1:29), everyone who will accept the light and truth that He brings.

He wore the crown of mockery so that His beloved disciples would, one day, wear a crown of glory. He accepted the robe of mockery so that His disciples would receive the robe of salvation. When the soldiers hail Him as King, as the Romans hailed Caesar, they are unconsciously acknowledging the truth. Jesus IS the King of the Jews, the Messiah-King, whom God had promised over many centuries to send them, and this is His coronation day. Certainly, things are upside down, as they needs must be in the world of darkness, where no one can "see" and therefore no one can understand what is going on. For John, it is the Gentiles who will, eventually, acknowledge the kingship of Jesus when their eyes have been opened after they have been born of the Spirit.

Scene 5: Behold the Man (19:4–8)

The coronation of Jesus proceeds on to the outer stage again, as the acknowledged (18:40) and crowned king is now presented to His people, dressed in His "royal" robes and with His crowned head, for their acclamation. Israel's long wait for their Messianic King has come to fruition, but in a most extraordinary way. As Pilate presents Jesus the king, he acknowledges His innocence again, and will do so a third time before he, too, "hands him over" to be crucified. Maybe in mockery, maybe in admiration at the quiet majesty and control of Jesus in such terrible circumstances, Pilate exclaimed: "Behold the man!" Surely even if they could not acknowledge His divine sonship, they could see that they had quite *a man* on their hands! Pilate was used to the violent cursing and cries of the scourged and condemned, and he must have been deeply moved and disturbed by the quiet peace of Jesus that nothing could shake. Not even brutalizing Him could take away His majestic presence and calm. It merely showed up the magnificence of the personality. But it disturbed Pilate, as we shall see.

The acclaim of the leaders is not homage for their king, but shouts for His death: "*Crucify Him*! *Crucify Him*!" Only five days before, the crowds in Jerusalem had acclaimed Jesus their messiah-King: "*Hosanna*! *Blessed is He who is coming in the name of the Lord. THE KING OF ISRAEL*" (12:13). It seemed then as if they knew that He was the heavenly man foretold by Daniel (7:13–14), now He is just "the man" Caiaphas wants to die for the people, and, moreover, this is Passover preparation day when the paschal lambs are to be killed. On the "above" level it is right for Jesus to die today for His own people and for all peoples (11:51–52). It is sad, though, that neither the presiding chief priests nor the people know that THIS EVENT is their Passover, for which the killing of the lambs is but the symbolic preparation.

Frustrated that his devious stratagems are getting him nowhere, Pilate cynically tells the Jews to crucify Him themselves (something he knows is despicable to them, and which they would never carry out even if they had the authority to do it), for *he knows that Jesus is innocent*. Here for the third time, the world authority has declared Jesus to be the INNOCENT Lamb they are about to sacrifice that day. The Jewish leaders declared that, "*We have a Law, and according to THAT LAW He ought to be put to death, because He has claimed to be Son of God.*" Jesus cannot be killed according to Roman Law because He is not a subversive, so the Jews demand that He be killed according to their Law. This is a psychological victory over Pilate, who was known to despise the Jews, and who had violated their customs previously, a thing not tolerated in Rome from provincial governors, who, for the sake of peace and political stability, were to co-operate with local customs. Jesus is to die because He claimed to be the beloved Son that in fact He was.

Pilate's fears increased at this point. This is John's way of stating that this man is deeply disturbed by the silent and peaceful prisoner who stands in aweful personal freedom as a political battle is waged over His head. It is ironic that the representative of the might of Rome is now reduced to the same fear before Jesus as the great Sanhedrin experienced earlier when they decided to get rid of Him (11:47–50). Neither Pilate nor the Sanhedrin can stand neutral before the embodiment of truth, a truth which will set them free if accepted (8:32) or will judge them if they reject it, as is demonstrated here.

Pilate's fears were probably multiple, as he would not want to kill a man just to quieten the situation, nor would he want Rome to discover that Barabbas was freed. Now his superstitions are raised at the possibility of Jesus being a "son of the gods", a title given to the Emperor, but a title also indicating the mysterious origins of Jesus. Truly this case is getting out of hand altogether. The irony of the scene is that Jesus has been proclaimed "King of the Jews", the messianic "Son of Man" and now "Son of God". As the trial proceeds the truth about Jesus is seen.

Scene 6: From Where (19:9–11)

Pilate went backstage to Jesus to question Him on his origins: "*Where do You come from?*" he asked. Luke 23:4–7 says that Pilate sent Jesus to Herod when he discovered that He was from his territory in Galilee. This was another vain attempt to free Him. Here John deals with the deeper mystery of Jesus' heavenly origins. Like His Kingdom, Jesus Himself comes "from above", but Pilate cannot understand this as he has rejected the truth. Like other unbelievers, he is only interested in the earthly geographical origins (6:42, 7:41–42, 9:29–30). Jesus was silent, since Pilate was not open to the truth that no one has power over Jesus. He alone can lay down His life and then take it up again (10:17–18).

Besides, the Hour has come for Jesus to lay down His life, and so the Father has permitted Pilate to have a role in this mystery. It is not Rome or Jerusalem that has power during this Passover, but the heavenly Father, whose will is being done by His Beloved Son (14:30–31). Just as Caiaphas prophesied because he was High Priest "in that year" (11:49), so Pilate just "happened" to be the Roman Governor that same year! In one last dramatic move the trial is up-ended as Jesus, the true judge, passes judgement on Pilate, who is less guilty of Jesus' death than is Caiaphas, who engineered it from the beginning, or Judas, the friend who betrayed Him.

Scene 7: Death Sentence (19:12–16)

The dreadful climax approaches with Pilate still anxious to set Jesus free but finding himself powerless before His ruthless foes. "Friend of Caesar" was the title given to trusted envoys of Rome, who wielded power in the name of the Emperor. Political pressure is put upon him now that he will be reported to Caesar if this "pretend-king" is allowed to go free. This would mean an investigation into the prefect's conduct in office, which Pilate could not risk, as his past misdemeanours would bring him severe punishment. Tiberias, the reigning Caesar, who lived like a recluse on the island of Capri, was paranoid about personal loyalty, and ruthless with any envoy denounced to him. It is now Pilate's life or Jesus' that must go. It is strange that Jesus, having already given His life in place of Barabbas', must now do the same to "save" Pilate.

Pilate capitulates, but in doing so will make the Jewish leaders pay the highest price for this life they demand. They can "have" Jesus if they renounce their nationalistic expectations for a Davidic Messisah-King who would be a political figure to save them from the might of Rome. If they renounce Jesus they MUST state who their real king is: . . . *Pilate had Jesus brought out, and seated him on the chair of judgement at a place called the Pavement* . . . John says that Pilate placed Jesus on the chair of judgement because He was the true judge and the case was now closing. He does not have to pronounce the verdict, as the Jews judge themselves when they declare: "*We have no king except Caesar.*" Passover was the traditional time for celebrating God's judgement on the world as they sang of His liberation of Israel. This Passover it was judgement for Israel, with their Messiah-King on the judgement seat.

To "get" Jesus the Jews have renounced the Lord as their king. It had been their boast all down the centuries that God alone was THEIR king, while other nations merely had earthly kings (Judges 8:23; 1 Samuel 8:7; 2 Samuel 7:11–16; Isaiah 26:13; Psalm 2:7, etc). The only person who could rule over God's people was someone raised up by God Himself. Now at this solemn moment of Passover, when all Israel celebrated its deliverance from slavery and the making of the Covenant with God, the Jewish leaders solemnly break the Covenant, thus putting themselves in slavery to the "world", as they declare

Caesar – the symbol of the realm of "below" – their king and lord, with the right to rule over them.

Truly their hatred of Jesus had taken them to lengths they could not have foreseen. And their renunciation of the Messiah is done as the Messiah-King sits on His throne of judgement, robed and crowned as their king. Nothing could be more public, more solemn, or more frightening in its consequences. For Israel THIS was the ultimate blasphemy, and yet on the level of "above" the death of Jesus will inaugurate the Messianic reign of God over the whole world, and usher in the New Covenant in the blood of Jesus, showing thereby that the sin of the world cannot prevent the will of God from being accomplished, for God alone has power in the real sense.

The breaking of Covenant is done at twelve noon, just as the priests begin to slaughter the Passover lambs in the Temple precincts. They are unaware of the REAL LAMB being slaughtered by them that day, and just as the shed blood of the Passover lamb had set the Israelites in Egypt free from physical slavery, so the shed blood of the Lamb of God that day would set all believers free from spiritual slavery to sin and the domination of the world, thus enabling them to live at the level of the Spirit and to glorify God by living a heavenly life on earth.

Execution of the King

John presents the death of Jesus with great dignity and reserve, omitting some distressful scenes related in the Synoptic gospels. Thus he creates a sense of silence and awe in a place where normally one would expect raucous noise (Matthew 27:39–44). His emphasis is on the death of the King of the Jews, and he demonstrates that Jesus is the master of His own destiny. He gave permission to His betrayer to begin this "night" (13:27). He controlled His own arrest (18:4–11). His trial turned out to be a proclamation of His kingship. Now He carries His cross like a royal banner to His enthronement on Calvary, His "lifting up". Like Isaac in Genesis 22:6, He willingly carries the wood of His sacrifice in obedience to His Father, thus showing that He is also the victim-sacrifice for sin, expressing His love for us to the utter limits of love (13:1). As scripture had foretold, Jesus was crucified between malefactors (Isaiah 53:12), but in John they do not speak, as all attention is focused on Jesus.

Pilate himself *wrote out a notice and had it fixed to the cross; it ran "Jesus the Nazarene, King of the Jews"*. It was written in the three main languages of the known world at that time, thus making a universal proclamation. Pilate must clear himself legally by fixing the notice of the "crime" to the cross, but unconsciously he is fixing the attention of the world to the cosmic nature of this event. The Jewish leaders object, for this looks as if a real Jewish king is being executed, but Pilate remains firm and refuses to be manipulated further. Not only will Rome be pleased with Pilate's dealings with Jewish kings, but the Father in heaven will too, as Pilate is the "authority" He chose to proclaim Jesus' kingship. Thus heaven and earth agree that Jesus is king! Now that He is being "lifted up" from the earth he will draw all peoples to Himself as His "subjects". It is FROM this throne that Jesus will save and rule the world (3:14–16, 12:32, 18:14).

Crucifixion (19:17–24)

As soon as we arrive on Golgotha we enter into the relative silence of the cross, where John gives five scenes to help us contemplate this awesome mystery. Gone now is the noise and flurry of the Praetorium as we watch the stripping of this extraordinary prisoner. This practice was another aspect of crucifixion desgined to humiliate the person. When Jesus was stripped of His clothes they found His undergarment was seamless, such as that worn by the High Priest. It was customary to give the belongings of the crucified to the soldiers on duty. They were reluctant to tear the garment into four, so, deciding to cast lots for it, they fulfilled the prophecy of Psalm 22:18: "*They divided my garments among them and cast lots for my clothes*."

In pointing out this seamless robe, John is proclaiming Jesus not only as king, but also as the High Priest of the New Covenant, thus showing that Jesus fulfilled in Himself everything that Judaism stood for. He is the High Priest "consecrating himself" as victim to undo the sin of the world (17:19), and to bring about the release of all its captives. This king-priest is the mediator between God and humankind, bringing all that the Passover represented to final fruition. Some claim that the untorn garment also represents the oneness of the Body of Believers who are united to Jesus and to each other.

Mother And Son (19:25–27)

Near the Cross of Jesus stood His mother and His mother's sister, Mary the wife of Clopas, and Mary of Magdala. Seeing His mother and the disciple whom He loved standing near her, Jesus said to His mother, "Woman, this is your son". Then to the disciple He said, "This is your mother". And from that hour the disciple took her into his home. This incident is unique to John. The Synoptics place the women with the disciples at a distance from the cross (Matthew 27:55–56; Mark 15:40; Luke 23:49), but John places Jesus' mother, and three other believing women, close to the cross unafraid of all the gore in their desire to be with Jesus in any way they could.

They are "with" Him physically, but also spiritually, as they enter into this mystery as deeply as they know how, letting their hearts guide, where the "head" cannot understand. In this way they will be "with" Jesus throughout His ordeal. They stand in awful contrast to the soldiers, who care nothing for the dying man, and to the chief priests who are responsible for His death. Thus those on the side of light and darkness are clearly represented at the cross, "doing" the works of light and darkness (3:20–21).

Jesus' response to His mother's presence has to be read on two levels. First, as an only child it was His duty to provide for His mother in a society that had no social protection for widows. If Jesus had brothers and sisters, giving His mother to someone outside the family would be inexplicable. One of the theories regarding the identity of the women at the cross suggests that "His mother's sister" may be the "Salome" who was the mother of the sons of Zebedee (a combination of Matthew 27:56 and Mark 15:40). If this were true, then Jesus gave His mother to His cousin John, a reasonable suggestion since John would be part of the family. (This presumes that John is the Beloved Disciple.)

However, John's interest is more theological. Jesus on the cross is the Messianic King who is about to make a final revelation regarding the future "home" of His beloved disciples. Mary, His mother, had intervened at Cana of Galilee to initiate His ministry, but was refused because His Hour had not yet come. Now the Hour is here, and the New Eve is given her role in the new age. Just as she mothered Jesus in His natural life, so now she is to mother Christians, represented by the Beloved Disciple. They are to accept Mary's mothering, and make their home with her "from that moment", meaning from the time of Jesus' Hour. Both mother and son are symbols of the Church which is "born" in the agony of Jesus' Hour (16:21–22).

Mary is the faithful Israelite who gave Jesus to Israel and to the world. She symbolizes the Church, the New Israel, Lady Zion, who will continue to bring the life of the Risen Jesus to all the world. Mother Zion gives birth to a new people in great pain, a people, unlike those of old, who

WILL bring forth the spirit of salvation upon the world (Isaiah 26:17–18). There will be great rejoicing at the birth of this new people (Isaiah 49:20–22, 54:1, 66:7–11; John 16:21). Her natural son is the first-born from the dead (see Colossians 1:18), the one who holds the keys of death and hell (see Revelation 1:18). All other members of this new people of God are "brothers" to Him and "children" to her.

As the Hour approaches consummation, when the heart of Jesus will be opened, Mary represents that New Eve who is being born from the side of the New Adam (Genesis 2:22). Like Eve she is called "woman" and the mother of all the living (Genesis 3:20), for Mary is now constituted the mother of all those who live in the Spirit. The Beloved Disciple is now a son of Mary and brother of Jesus, part of the family who do the will of God (14:15, 23, 15:10). Like Eve, the community of believers, who constitute the new Church, will also be involved in the struggle with Satan (Genesis 3:15). When the evil one fails to destroy Mary's first-born, he will proceed to vent his anger and hatred on the rest of her children, the New People of God (Revelation: 12:5, 17).

The Beloved Disciple is given a new role also. He is to care for Mary and take her to his home. Tradition tells us that John, the son of Zebedee, did in fact take Mary with him to Ephesus, where he was the leader of the Church. But the meaning here is deeper than that. Since Mary represents the Church, the community of believers, this disciple is told to look after it. As a disciple he receives the life of the Risen Jesus in and through the Church. In return he is to care for the Church, which he did in his leadership role, and also in providing his witness to Jesus in this gospel. But this disciple represents Christians in general, who are told by Jesus to look after His community in the ages to come.

It Is Finished (19:28–30)

With the creation of the new Church Jesus knows that His work is complete. All that is left is for Him to cry out His thirst, and breathe forth His spirit in perfect love. Death by crucifixion produced a racking thirst that was dreadful to see, so the soldiers sometimes gave the dying man a drugged drink or some of their own sour wine (Matthew 27:48; Mark 15:23; Luke 23:36). But John is speaking at a deeper level, where the Beloved Son is eager to drink the Father's cup to the dregs, to show His love to the end (18:11). The scriptures had foretold that the people would not understand this thirst and would give Him the sedative or sour wine as a result (Psalm 69:11, 22:15). The misunderstanding of Jesus Himself and of what He stood for, goes right to the end of His life and beyond. Jesus knows that drinking this cup to the dregs is the price He must pay to provide the living waters to all those who are thirsty for God (7:37–39). In fact, in a few moments from now the living water will begin to flow from His opened heart.

The hyssop used to give this drink to Jesus is a deliberate statement on John's part, to remind us that Jesus is the Lamb of God dying to give life to the world. In the first Passover in Egypt, Moses ordered the hyssop stick to be used to sprinkle the blood of the Paschal Lamb on the doorposts of any house where the occupants wanted to be saved. John is reminding us, *as Jesus dies*, that it is His precious blood that saves us from our sins. (It would be more normal for the soldier to use a lance to give the vinegar to Jesus.)

Now that all things have been fulfilled to the letter, Jesus announces that the work given to Him by the Father is finished, and He is free to return to the Father from whom He came. Without any desolate cry such as the Synoptics relate, Jesus here dies with the same calm determined majesty of one in complete control of the situation. He dies when HE is ready, when all scripture has been accomplished, not when His enemies would desire it. His death is, therefore, a triumph – for Him, for love, and for the Father's plan of salvation. He has laid down His life for His sheep as He promised. But in the laying down of His life, He poured forth His Spirit on the new community being born through His death. His Spirit is yielded up to those whom He loves, who are represented by those at the foot of the cross, so that from now on they, too, can live in the Spirit, and on the level of "above". He will hand over His Spirit officially in the resurrection (20:22).

Strike the Rock (19:31–37)

The silence and quiet sense of awe continues after Jesus' death. Even though there is need for haste because the great Feast is about to begin, and it is a specially solemn one in that this time it is a Sabbath, the atmosphere remains reverent and solemn. John does not relate the apocalyptic events that accompanied the death of Jesus (Matthew 27:51–54; Mark 15:38–39; Luke 23:44–48). He prefers, as usual, to look into the deeper significance of simple events that would otherwise have been overlooked or misunderstood. Jesus has entered into God's eternal Sabbath, the rest He earned after His labours on behalf of others, the rest that symbolizes the Promised Land (Letter to Hebrews 3:7–4:11).

Crucifixion was a slow death that often took several days, for the soldiers would not normally damage any vital organ, and the person eventually died of thirst, exposure, and finally suffocation. It was normal for the Romans to leave the body on the cross as a warning to any would-be offenders, but this practice was abhorrent to the Jews. They would not leave a man hanging overnight, as such a person was considered accursed in God's sight, so the Jews demanded that death be hastened in this case by breaking the legs, thus bringing on suffocation quickly (Deuteronomy 21:23; Galatians 3:13). Rome permitted this practice, so permission was given by Pilate. They broke the legs of the men who were crucified with Jesus, but when they came to Him, they saw that He was already dead, so they did not touch Him. John brings out the significance of this by quoting Exodus 12:46, a reminder that Jesus is the Paschal Lamb, and it was laid down that: *Not one bone of His will be broken* (see also Psalm 34:20; Numbers 9:12).

Jesus' side was then jabbed and pierced by a soldier in an attempt to certify that He was dead. And testifies to a miracle: . . . *and immediately there flowed out blood and water*. This needed eye-witness testimony, and the disciple behind this gospel puts all the weight of his authority into that. Why? Because Jesus is not only the sacrificial Lamb, but He is also the Rock that Moses struck in the desert to provide water for the thirsty people of God (Numbers 20:11): "Moses then raised his hand and struck the rock twice with the branch; water gushed out in abundance . . ." In 1 Corinthians 10:4 Paul says: " . . . they drank from the spiritual rock which followed them, and that rock was Christ." John has already told us in 7:38–39 that Jesus intended giving the fountains of Living Water, which represent the overflowing gift of the Spirit, but only after His death (16:7). Now the "rock of our salvation" has been struck and the living waters flow to all thirsty souls.

Another aspect is that Jesus' body IS the New Temple (2:20–22). The prophet Ezekiel (47:1–12) had foreseen the river of life flowing from the right-hand side of the Temple, giving abundant fruitfulness to anyone who lived by its waters. Revelation 22:1–2 sees the fulfilment of this prophecy in the Lamb of God, so those who live by these abundant waters are those who bring forth the fruit of the Spirit that Jesus asked of His followers (John 15).

The miracle was a flow of blood and water. The blood signifies that Jesus' death was life-giving for all (1 John

5:6–8). The blood of the sacrificial lamb had to be poured over the altar, and sprinkled on the people. Thus John testifies that the precious blood of Jesus did, in fact, pour over the new altar, which is His own body, as a life-giving stream for the salvation of all. Later centuries saw symbols of the two most important sacraments here, the life-blood of the Church. The water represents Baptism, whereby a person becomes a member of the people of God, and the blood the Eucharist, which is their daily spiritual food.

Burial (19:38–42)

One of the prophecies that John sees fulfilled in Jesus' death is that of Zechariah 12:10, in which the prophet said that one day God would pour out a spirit of prayer and grace on Jerusalem, and that they would look on the one they had pierced and mourn for him as for an only child who was the first-born. Somehow this piercing would open their eyes to the reality of who was in their midst. This appears to have happened in the case of two distinguished men of high rank who were hidden during the time of the ministry and only came forward after the death of Jesus. They were Joseph of Arimathea, a prince, and Nicodemus, a member of the great Sanhedrin. They used their privileged position in society to secure the body of Jesus, and took charge of the burial, thus securing maximum honour for this crucified "criminal".

It would be normal custom to bury the bodies in a common grave near the execution site. We are not told what happened to the two malefactors who died with Jesus, just that Jesus was buried in a special tomb, with all honour, just like a king. The final act after death was the *binding* of the body of Jesus in the burial cloths, which eloquently illustrates the destructive power of sin in the cosmos, seeking to bind and to kill – but Jesus will undo this binding and will conquer death. They hastily laid Him in the tomb with large quantities of spices, myrrh and aloes to keep the body fresh and sweet-smelling as long as possible.

And so the Beloved Son is laid to rest as the solemn Sabbath is announced. How little they understand what a Sabbath it is, that this is God's Sabbath, His rest after the labour of Redemption, and what glory awaits them as the New Moses goes ahead to the Promised Land preparing the way, all the way back to the Father's house for anyone who wants to come.

Chapter 20
Dawn of the New Era

There is such a break between the last chapter, where Jesus is brutalized and killed, and this one, that one needs to stop a while and think. Jerusalem celebrated the great Sabbath, which was also Passover in that year, without realizing that its final fulfilment took place before their unseeing eyes. Neither do they know that a man has re-entered Paradise to begin the eternal Sabbath of God's reign. Only now in this present chapter will some Israelites come to understand that the lifting up of Jesus on the cross was the preliminary to His being lifted up in glory. The veil between heaven and earth had been torn apart before the Sabbath began (Matthew 27:51), and Jesus entered the heavenly sanctuary as priest and victim on behalf of us all, taking His own precious blood with Him to atone for our sins, opening up access to God for everyone (Letter to Hebrews, chapter 9), and sealing the New Covenant on our behalf.

All this happened silently and lovingly as the "world" is bathed in darkness and unbelief, and in seeming "victory". As Jesus had predicted (16:20), that Sabbath was one of suffering for the disciples, for they had guilt added to the mourning, in the memory of having deserted Jesus in His hour of need (Mark 16:10). Now as we approach the dawn of the new eternal day, when Light triumphs over darkness, Life over death, victory over failure; when the veil separating us from the unseen world of the realm of "above" is suddenly taken away, we are, like the disciples and the women, taken by surprise and we cannot cope. The timelessness of eternity breaks in upon us, and we are confronted by the inexplicable.

Like the other evangelists, John decided to present this mystery in his own way, leaving out some dramatic events told by the Synoptists. He concentrates on how the witnesses came to believe in the resurrection of Jesus. At no time does he set out to "prove" that the resurrection really happened. One is expected to "see" in the transformation of the witnesses, as they travel from blindness to "seeing and believing", as the risen glory of Jesus breaks in upon their lives, transforming them from fearful, half-understanding disciples, to fearless witnesses prepared to lay down their lives in testimony to the glorious victory of their Lord.

The Great Discovery (20:1–10)

It was Sunday, the first of the Christian Era, when darkness was still apparently reigning, that Mary of Magdala went to the tomb of Jesus to mourn for Him. This was the moment of stillness before the inrush of glory and joy. "My Beloved is the tranquil night before the rising of the dawn" (St John of the Cross).

It was customary to visit a tomb for three days after a death, so Mary's visit is not in expectation of anything, but just a last sign of love from this incredible lover of Jesus, who in response to His gift of forgiveness and new life became a disciple unto death for Him. On arrival she found that the tomb was open, with the stone which sealed it rolled back. Matthew's gospel says that the chief priests had put a seal on the stone and guards protecting the tomb, for fear the disciples would steal the body (Matthew 27:62–66). The sight of the opened tomb did not fill Mary with joy, but with the horrible thought of grave robbers. She did not investigate, but presumed the most obvious thing. Resurrection was the last thing on her mind. She ran to Peter and the Beloved Disciple with the terrible news, and her message implies that she was not alone as the

Synoptics relate (Matthew 28:1; Mark 16:1; Luke 24:1–8): "*They have taken the Lord out of the tomb*," *she said*, "*and WE don't know where they have put Him*."

Horror and dismay sent Peter and the beloved disciple running to the tomb to investigate. That Peter is still the undisputed leader is seen in the response of Mary and the beloved disciple to him. Deference is shown, and he is allowed to enter the tomb first to confront the evidence: . . . *saw the linen cloths lying on the ground and also the cloth that had been over His head; this was not with the linen cloths but rolled up in a place by itself*. Some translators do not say that the cloths were on the ground, but just lying there where the body had been. When Jesus rose from the dead He left the grave cloths behind, as He had no further need of the trappings of earth (see Romans 6:9). When Lazarus rose from the dead he was wrapped in the grave cloths as he would have to die again, but Jesus was clothed in glory because death was conquered for ever.

The scene that confronted the two men (for John entered after Peter), was not theft, as grave robbers would need the body well wrapped up for their foul purposes. The normality of the scene before them was amazing: someone had got up and just left the place untidy as he left. These are the facts: how do we relate to them? John does not tell us that Peter went back puzzled (Luke 24:12), but that the beloved disciple *saw and he believed*. The one who had the deepest relationship to Jesus in love, was the first to break into the mystery of the resurrection. What the head could not grasp was understood by the heart. Love is the key to breaking into the realm of "above", which has begun now on this day. While Peter had the primacy in terms of leadership, the beloved disciple had the primacy in love, and the insight that love gives into the things of God. It was this that enabled them to penetrate the scriptures afterwards and realize that Jesus fulfilled them as the whole gospel testifies.

The Problem of Recognition (20:11–18)

All the gospels relate stories of the problem the disciples had in recognizing the risen Jesus. We are told that He was REALLY there present to them, yet He was different to the point that they found difficulty in recognizing Him at first, even though He still bore the marks of the wounds (20:25), and ate and drank in their presence (Luke 24:42), thus showing that He certainly was neither a ghost (Luke 24:39) nor a spiritual vision. But how to explain His presence? It WAS really Jesus, but so transformed in glory that His body had different qualities that were not bound to time and space (20:19; 1 Corinthians 15:42–58). John's recognition stories are those of Mary and Thomas, and he uses both to bring out the continuing revelation of who Jesus is, how He dwells among us, and how He kept the promise He made in the Final Discourse.

Mary was standing outside the tomb, weeping. Then she looked inside and saw two angels sitting where the body of Jesus had lain. They asked her why she was weeping, since this was not a day for mourning but for rejoicing, but Mary has yet to enter into the mystery before she, too, can rejoice. She explained that her sorrow was over the loss of Jesus' body, a loss that made her mourning unbearable. Mary is unimpressed by the angelic visitors. Her need is for Jesus; nobody else can replace Him, alive or dead. Suddenly she became aware of someone approaching from behind. She turned and found Jesus standing in front of her. Gently drawing her from her mourning, Jesus asked whom she was looking for. As we have already seen, this is the all-important question which will lead to faith in His resurrection. Mary's sorrow is such that she has no time for conversation. She only has time for the one she loves, so presuming that He is the gardener she enquired whether he had taken the body! (John appears to be answering some objectors in his own day, who said that perhaps the gardener had stolen the body of Jesus.)

Mary has been a good disciple up to now, so the Shepherd calls His sheep by name. She hears His voice, and recognizing the voice of the shepherd, she throws herself at his feet, clinging to him in pure joy (10:3, 14, 15). She had clung to Him in life, she had clung to Him in death, and now she clings to Him in the resurrection. What constancy! It was the voice of the Shepherd in her heart that opened her eyes to recognize Him in the new mode of His existence. He had, indeed, taken the body, and in doing so had taken the sting out of death, for when He left the tomb He left the door open. Death was never again to be the end of anyone's life (1 Corinthians 15:54–57), because Jesus had fulfilled Psalm 126. In His saving death, He had delivered Zion's captives, so that now the redeemed have their mouths filled with laughter and song when they realize what the Lord has done. He left them on Friday sowing the tears of His martyrdom; today He comes back with the sheaves of victory. Today sinners should rejoice in their deliverance.

Mary said to Jesus: "Rabbuni!" which means "My beloved Master!" Jesus replied: "*Do not cling to Me, because I have not yet ascended to the Father. But go and* find My brothers, *and tell them*: *I am ascending to My Father and your Father, to My God and your God*." Mary's words of recognition to Jesus would seem to be an early stage in faith, as it was early in the ministry that they called Jesus "Rabbi" or teacher, yet John here says it means "Master", which they did call Him throughout. Yet she refers to Jesus twice as "The Lord" (verses 13 and 18), the title used after the resurrection.

As Mary clings to Jesus the words of the Psalmist ring out again with a special newness: *You have turned my mourning into dancing, you have stripped off my sackcloth and clothed me with joy. So my heart will sing to you unceasingly, O Lord, my God, I shall praise you forever* (Psalm 30:11–12). Mary also echoes the bride in the Song of Songs

(3:1–4), who went out into the city looking for her beloved and could not find him. She enquired of the watchmen whether they had seen Him, when suddenly she saw Him herself, clung to Him and would not let Him go. Here she exemplifies the search of the individual disciple for Jesus. That person must persevere in seeking Him and be put off by nothing, nor must they accept a lesser revelation as seen in the angelic presence. The disciples must not rest until they find Jesus Himself. The key to finding Him is to listen in prayer, and to the Word of God, for there the Shepherd is speaking and calling each one to Himself.

Kneeling at the Master's feet is a sign of openness to Him and to whatever He asks of us. If the clinging is true, we will do His bidding. Jesus asks Mary to let go of the Jesus she knew last week in order to receive Him back in a new way. Openness to the Lord implies that we hold life lightly and that we are ready to move on. If Mary insists on having the Jesus of "before Passover" she will never know the cosmic Christ, nor can she participate in His worldwide mission. He is in transit to the Father. His lifting up in glory is under way, and she must let Him go, being glad that she no longer sees Him with the eyes of flesh, for she will see Him with the eyes of the Spirit. If she accepts to let Him go, then she will receive Him back in permanent indwelling, as He promised. There He is no longer tied to time and space as He was in the incarnation. She will understand Him better when the gift of the Spirit has been poured forth upon the believing community.

She is also asked to leave this place where she has found her Easter joy, for she must become a missionary in His name. The resurrection must be proclaimed to everyone. No one is allowed to stay clinging to their own joy. It must be shared, so Mary is commissioned to become an apostle to the beloved disciples, and to announce Easter glory to the men whom Jesus refers to as "My brothers" because they have now been born of God and they constitute His new family in the spirit. Mary's Easter proclamation is pure joy: "I am ascending to My Father and your Father, to My God and your God." They can now claim to be sons of God and brothers of Jesus and of each other, and live in the realm of divine love, where the Spirit of God will be their guide from now on.

Jesus' words are similar to those of Ruth to her mother-in-law, Naomi: "*Where you go, I shall go, wherever you live, I shall live. Your people will be my people, and your God will be my God*" (Ruth 1:16). Jesus is telling Mary that as she walks away from her present meeting with Him, she will "have" Him in an altogether new way. In fact, because of His indwelling her, He will go with her wherever she goes, and He will live within her whatever land she finds herself in. Not only is He released from the barriers of time and space, but she is also, as she steps out onto the level of "above" with its limitless possibilities. Now she realizes what "worshipping the Father in spirit and truth" is. There is no need for a temple building, for the beloved disciples ARE the Temple of God, where the Holy Spirit lives and works, continuing the ministry of Jesus. Mary then walked away in freedom from the visible presence of Jesus that was no longer necessary for her walk in faith, and she proclaimed the resurrection to the disciples as she had been told.

He Came! (20:19–23)

Easter Day saw the disciples locked behind closed doors for fear of arrest from the Sanhedrin. *Jesus came and stood among them. He said to them, "Peace be with you", and, after saying this, He showed them His hands and His side.* Luke 24:36–39 says that they were in a state of alarm at the realization that Jesus had come in through closed doors, a fact that confronted them with the newness of His risen state. Then He showed them His wounds as proof that it was really Himself, and that He had returned to them as He had promised (14:19) to bring them His own peace (14:27) and joy (15:11) that would be permanent from now on.

He will also bestow upon them the gift of His Spirit, which could only be given after He had been lifted up (16:7). In this way they will have the enduring presence of Jesus, and the gift of divine sonship which is the basis of Christian peace (14:20). Their joy at seeing the Lord fulfils Jesus' own prophecy in 16:21, where He told them that after a period of intense suffering they would know great joy at the realization that a man had been born to the risen life, thus opening the way to all others. As believers in the Old Covenant, the disciples knew that the gifts of peace and joy were promised as the end-time graces, when God would have restored all things according to His plan. Revelation 19:7 and 21:1–4 show its final fulfilment at the Second Coming of Jesus in glory.

It seems from Luke's account that the disciples are having a meal (24:42). It is interesting, therefore, that John evokes the memories of that last famous meal they had with Jesus, when He gave them his Final Discourse. In a similar context that must have jolted their memories, He fulfils all that He promised there, and so soon after it. John also omits the stress on the Twelve (Eleven now), speaking instead of "disciples", which allows him to demonstrate here the gift of the Spirit which was given to a greater number of Jesus' followers, as we see in Acts 2. All the gifts given by Jesus here are for disciples in general. It is their Christian heritage.

Christians know that the risen Lord is with them in such a way that no persecution can stop Him from reaching them. There are no earthly "doors" that can block His presence, now that He has entered the timelessness of "the other side". Christians should not fear persecution then, when their Lord is with them, strengthening them by His Spirit, and giving them the wisdom they need to deal with all circumstances. And this unseen presence of Jesus in His believing community IS THE SAME Jesus who displayed His wounds before His aghast witnesses on Easter Day.

Now comes the solemn moment of their commissioning as His sent-agents, apostles. "*As the Father sent Me, so I am sending you.*" Here the risen Lord entrusts the worldwide mission to these disciples, and those in the future who represent them. They are to be sent in exactly the same way as the Father sent the Son, with all authority to teach, preach and work miracles, taking those who are spiritually and physically dead and raising them to new life. Just as the mission of the Son continued the Father's work on earth (5:17), so the disciples will continue the mission of Jesus. This requires that the Son be present to them on mission, as the Father was present to the Son (12:45).

From now on whoever sees the beloved disciples is seeing Jesus (13:20). Jesus will live in them through His Spirit. Jesus had prayed at the Last Supper that His disciples would be consecrated or made holy by the truth, which is Jesus' word, and for this purpose He went to His Hour so that He could bestow on them the Holy Spirit of truth. The sending forth of the disciples, then, is bound up with the sending forth of the Spirit. Once they receive the Spirit they can bring life and salvation to others who believe (6:57), and they can bestow this gift of the Spirit on others.

After saying this He breathed on them and said: "*Receive the Holy Spirit. If you forgive anyone's sins, they are forgiven; if you retain anyone's sins, they are retained.*" Just as God had breathed life into the lifeless form of Adam in Genesis 2:7, a form that was created and ready for the gift of life, so, Jesus having created His new community on Calvary, this new being is ready to receive the gift of the Spirit that will enable it to rise from its non-life of unbelief to become the new people of God in the New Testament (Wisdom 15:11). The New Creation has now received the gift of eternal life, and is born of the Spirit, making them the family of God. The life of the Father flowing through Jesus is now flowing through them, fulfilling John 3:5. The desired day of the Coming of God's Spirit has come, so the end-time is now!

There are echoes of the vision of Ezekiel in the valley of the dry bones, when the prophet, who was called "son of man", was asked to prophesy to these bones and cause them to live. Here the REAL Son of Man, back from the dead, breathes into the lifeless community and causes it to rise and become the people of God. The marvel of the resurrection is such that it is not only essential for Jesus to rise, but it is essential for US to rise with Him to newness of life (Colossians 3:1–4). These disciples now become "brothers" to Jesus as they are born to God the Father.

"*Receive the Holy Spirit. If you forgive anyone's sins, they are forgiven; if you retain anyone's sins, they are retained.*" Now that the "new man" or the New Creation is formed, they are commissioned as the Son had been, to go into the unbelieving cosmos and UNBIND everyone, so that others could throw off the gravecloths of sin and attachment to the ways of the world and its false value system, and stand up and live in the spirit. The raising of the dry bones must continue through the ministry of the disciples. To this end they are empowered to forgive sin, thus bestowing peace and joy on others. The dreadful responsibility that rests on the community of Jesus is the fact that HE SAYS that if we retain people's sins they ARE retained. That means that if we refuse to let them go free, we hold them bound in sin and under the judgement of God. The unbinding of Jesus in the Resurrection, which freed Him from the clutches of death, signifies the beginning of the unbinding of the world from the clutches of sin that leads to the REAL death, which is hell. The tomb is open, so why not walk free?

There is a further aspect to the forgiveness of sin that deserves mention, namely that the community of believers continue the work of Jesus through His Spirit. This involves facing the world with its sin and wrong judgements, and convicting it (15:26–27, 16:8). But we have already seen that their ministry will receive the same acceptance as His, so that involves the rejection of the Word, and the ministry, and THIS leaves those people in their sin, for they have rejected the means of salvation provided for them (9:39–41). The light will continue to shine through the disciples' discriminating between those who accept and come to forgiveness, and those who reject, who go away hardened in their blindness. The Church not only provokes repentance by her preaching but also mediates the forgiveness of Jesus to repentant sinners, both at Baptism and beyond. The unbinding continues throughout our lives.

My Lord and My God! (20:24–29)

Thomas, who was one of the Twelve, had not been present at the first "showing" of Jesus. He refused to accept the word of the other witnesses, who kept telling him that Jesus was risen, and that they had seen Him. Thus John introduces us to a problem that arose towards the close of the apostolic age, namely, how could one believe in the resurrection if one had not seen the Lord? What about all those Christians who would have to accept the testimony from the lips of others, without being in a position to "prove" it for themselves? John answers this question with his usual drama, and in doing so responds to those Christians who demand signs and wonders before they believe (4:48).

Thomas replied: "*Unless I can see the holes that the nails made in His hands and can put my finger into the holes they made, and unless I can put my hand into His side I REFUSE to believe.*" He demands scientific evidence for the resurrection. His arrogance and pride should not be missed. He probably thought he was being clever, but his words indicate that he was NOT thinking of Jesus as the great I AM, or else this irreverence would be unthinkable. He demands MORE than the chief witnesses in the believing community, which was probably the problem being dealt with in the second half of the first century when the gospel was being written. He refuses to accept that Jesus is invisibly among them. He wants to probe the miraculous for himself, and on the basis of his own findings to decide whether to believe or not.

A week later, a very humble Jesus came to the gathered community with Thomas present. He invited Thomas to come forward and examine His wounds: "*Put your finger here*; *look*, *here are My hands. Give Me your hand*; *put it into My side. DO NOT BE UNBELEVING ANY MORE but believe.*" *Thomas replied*, "*My Lord and my God*!" Unbelief is what keeps people from penetrating the glory of the risen Jesus, and unbelief was behind Thomas' arrogant demands. Seeing Jesus and His wounds was enough for Thomas, who appears not to have touched the body of Jesus at all. The sight of His glory changed everything (17:5), and Thomas slipped to his knees and gave the final statement of this gospel about Jesus: "My Lord and my God!" words which up to this moment had been said to God alone (Psalm 35:23). But now is the time for all to honour the Son as they honour the Father (5:23). Now is the time to recognize in Jesus the great I AM, as He promised they would after He had been lifted up (8:28). Now they see the Father in Him (14:9).

At the beginning of the gospel many titles were given to Jesus: Rabbi (1:49), Prophet (4:19), Messiah (4:26), Saviour of all the world (4:42), Holy One (6:69), Son of Man (9:37), Son of God (11:27), King of the Jews (18:39), but to say that Jesus is the incarnation of God is the very reason why the gospel was written. It began with the statement that "The Word was God" and it finishes with the adoration of the Christian community: "My Lord and my God!" Here Thomas speaks for all believers.

Jesus said to him: "*You believe because you can see Me. Blessed are those who have not seen and yet believe*." This comment of Jesus is both sad and wonderful, sad because He was saying that Thomas' own converts, who would believe on the strength of HIS WORD ALONE, were more blessed in God's sight than he himself was, who refused to believe on the strength of the apostolic witness. Mature faith, for John, is based in the person of Jesus alone, not on signs and wonders, and it would be the common experience of all Christians after the apostolic age to believe without seeing. Thus John replies to objections that the original disciples were sort of "first class" since they had seen the Lord after He rose from the dead. Perhaps Christians were beginning to demand personal experience of the risen Lord before they would believe? Accepting His unseen presence in the Body of Believers was not enough for them, and they began to demand scientific evidence.

A new type of faith was demanded after the Ascension of Jesus. The original believers had seen the Lord, but that would no longer pertain. Jesus was concerned for future believers when He prayed for them in 17:20, those who would believe on the word of the disciples alone. Thus Jesus comforts all future believers who would be the fruit of the mission of the disciples (1 Peter 1:8).

Conclusion (20:30–31)

In conclusion John explains the motive for writing his gospel. It is an essential part of the apostolic witness for all future believers. The original witnesses did not leave the message to be passed on by word of mouth alone. They left us an official testimony in the written gospel, on which they expect us to base our belief in Jesus. An interesting point is that John says that it is not necessary to know every detail of the life and ministry of Jesus in order to receive the full benefits that He came to bring us. He deliberately left out some of the available material, selecting from it those events that helped him present his witness best.

This IS the WORD on which we are to believe, and John puts the weight of his authority behind his statement that if we DO believe on the strength of HIS witness then we, too, *may have life through His name*. Two thousand years on, and still the living waters flow from this Fount of Life.

Chapter 21
Meeting in Galilee

The Risen Lord (21:1–14)

This chapter follows the conclusion to the gospel, and commentators feel that its author must have been a disciple of John who wanted to deal with the reality of the resurrection, and the relative positions of Peter and the Beloved Disciple in the later Church. Obviously some people were saying that the disciples had only seen a vision of Jesus, that He was not really there, that it was merely something that their excited minds conjured up in their need to have Jesus back. To answer this, the present author went back into the tradition which had evidence of a meeting with Jesus by the Lake of Tiberias some time after the events of Easter. John had admitted in 20:30 that there were many other signs that Jesus gave which he chose not to relate. It is one of these that is dealt with now (Mark 16:7; Matthew 28:16–20).

A group of six disciples under Peter's leadership went out fishing by night, which was the best time to go, and headed back for shore tired, having caught nothing. They worked throughout the darkness of the night, and just as dawn was breaking they noticed a man on the shore, who, seeing their dejection, asked whether they had caught anything. Then, mysteriously, he directed them to catch a huge quantity of fish. The basic story is so simple yet packed with theological meaning.

Later on, Jesus revealed Himself again to the disciples. It was by the Sea of Tiberias, and it happened like this. This story is about Jesus revealing Himself: " . . . *that life was made visible; we saw it and are giving our testimony . . .*" (1 John 1:2). John the Baptist had revealed Jesus to the disciples at the beginning of the gospel (1:31), when some of those present in this incident were involved – Peter, the sons of Zebedee, Nathanael . . . The author wants to connect the beginning of the gospel with this final revelation, so that the disciples will know who Jesus really is, and see the whole gospel as one piece of testimony.

Jesus continued this revelation through His signs (2:11), His greatest sign being the resurrection. It is there that they finally see Him as Lord. Nathanael had been promised greater things at the beginning (1:50), now he can see them come to light in the risen glory of Jesus, and the miracle of the New Israel of which he is part. The revelation they receive of Jesus today is the culmination of all they have received up to now, and preparation for His final return in glory in the Parousia (see 1 John 3:2; 1 Peter 5:4; Colossians 3:4).

The fishing expedition with Peter in charge symbolizes the mission they had received "to catch people" (Luke 5:11). But they must remember that Jesus said "without Me you can do nothing" (15:5). It is a waste of time for them to try to bring forth the fruit of the Kingdom without Jesus. Out there in the unbelieving world "it is night", which only the light of Jesus' presence can penetrate. Jesus alone can "draw all men to Himself" now that He has been lifted up (12:32). The light of dawn was already present before they even saw that there was someone there. It took the sign of the marvellous catch of fish to enable them to discern that "presence" to be Jesus Himself. Only He could produce such a sign, as they well knew, and it jogs their memories of past signs. Nevertheless, recognition is not immediate.

The one who had the primacy in love recognized Jesus first. The beloved disciple exclaimed: "*It is the Lord*!" As we have already pointed out, love is the key to understanding Him who is Love Incarnate. Peter, who had the primacy in leadership, quickly tied his outer cloak around him and jumped into the sea to swim ashore. He, too, loved Jesus, as his impetuosity shows. Greeting an important person was considered a religious act, so Peter would not go to Jesus dressed only in the loin cloth that fishermen wore out at sea. He swam the hundred yards to shore while the others brought in the boat with its haul of fish.

When they arrived Jesus had a charcoal fire burning, and breakfast cooking on it. He asked for some of the catch too. The charcoal fire is a reminder to us, if not to Peter, that the last time this disciple met Jesus, he stood by a charcoal fire and denied that he ever knew Him (18:18). But things are different between them now, as we shall see. In obedience to Jesus, Peter dragged the net, with its haul of fish, ashore. Even though there were one hundred and fifty-three fish there the net was not broken. What a sign for them!

The whole scene describes Peter in charge of the mission, with the other disciples co-operating with him. The harvest is great because Jesus is with the believing community through His indwelling, His Word, and in the Eucharist, symbolized by the breakfast He prepared for them. The unbroken net signifies the oneness of the Body of Christ, as we have seen in the untorn garment of Jesus on Calvary (19:24). The exact quantity of fish has been variously interpreted, but represents the fullness of the harvest won for God by the believing community. It indicates that no matter how many come to Christ with their variety and diversity, there is plenty of room for them (14:2). The Church can hold them without schism (Matthew 28:19), because Jesus is the Lord of unity and the creator of community.

Jesus said to them, "*Come and have breakfast.*" *None of the disciples was bold enough to ask*, "*Who are you?*"; *they knew quite well it was the Lord*. If the author is pointing out the reality of the resurrection, he does so by showing us that a "vision" or a "ghost" would not point out a shoal of fish to a group of fishermen, or make breakfast on a charcoal fire, and certainly not sit down and join them. He is saying so clearly that the Jesus they knew was *really there*, but His transformed body made Him look different. He was the same, yet different. They did not know how to relate to someone come back from the dead, so they are awestruck and shy in His presence.

He lets them know that He is present in their Eucharistic gatherings, not only AT the meal but IN the meal, of which this present one is a symbol. From now on the challenge of every disciple is to recognize Him in the fellowship meal, the breaking of bread (Luke 24:31). This meal of bread and fish is the same as at the multiplication of the loaves (6:11), where He had shown them the two breads that would feed the spiritual hunger of the people, the bread of His Word (6:35–51) and the bread of the Eucharist (6:52–58). They must teach their flock to look beyond the bread they eat to discern the presence of their saving Lord.

Thus a summary of Jesus' various "presences" is given, and it reminds the disciples to perceive Him in the miraculous success of their mission, in their "diversity in unity"; to find Him in their preaching of the Word, in the Eucharist, as well as His indwelling in the hearts of each one. In this way it will no longer be necessary to have "appearances" of the risen Lord to enhance belief. That was only necessary at the beginning when the Church was coming into being. Jesus invites, not only the first disciples, but all disciples, to "come and eat", and in so doing recognize Him in their midst. All disciples, then, are called to the missionary task, to unity in community and to Eucharist.

A New Shepherd (21:15–19)

Luke's gospel (24:34) records a resurrection appearance to Simon Peter alone on Easter Day, but like Paul (1

Corinthians 15:5) he gives no details of what happened. It seems that here we are allowed into that private meeting to experience Jesus' forgiveness and love for this impetuous but loving disciple. It is one thing to receive forgiveness privately from Jesus, but it is an entirely different matter to be rehabilitated into one's former position in the community.

To forgive not only means to let the other person go free, but it also entails trusting them again, and this is the difficult part. Peter had betrayed Jesus' trust in him as the chief disciple when he cursed and swore that he never knew Him (Mark 14:71). In this scene Jesus restores him to his former position, while publicly and formally installing him as chief shepherd of the Flock of God. Forgiveness is one of the most attractive faces of Love, and Jesus demonstrates His own forgiving heart here to those present. The experience of forgiveness will make a good shepherd out of Peter, making him compassionate towards the Flock.

Three times, in front of the others, Jesus solemnly challenges Peter's love. No one but Jesus knew that Simon had "died" that night he denied his Lord. He was caught up in that awful "night" when people trip because they do not see their way forward (11:10). The question must be settled now as to whether this disciple has risen from that "death" to the realm of divine Love, with its limitless possibilities for personal growth and fruitfulness on mission.

Love is the key to the Kingdom of God, and so it is the subject on which he is questioned by Jesus now. "*Simon, son of John, do you love me MORE than these others do*?" The others would have thought that Peter loved Jesus less, for they had not sinned as much as he had. They had forgotten the teaching of Jesus, that those who have been forgiven much also love much in return (Luke 7:47). Jesus wants the new community to trust Peter's love for Him again, for HE knows that Peter does love Him more than the others do, that Peter is now ready to lay down his life for his Master, first in loving service to the Flock, and then in crucifixion.

Before his fall, when relying on his own strength, Peter had boasted that he would give his life for Jesus (13:38; Luke 22:34). There is no boast now as he appeals to Jesus' supernatural knowledge to prove that he loves Him. Relentlessly, Jesus pushes him, as he questions him three times to draw from him the pathetic response: "*Yes, Lord, you know I love you.*" He omits any comparison with the others, concerned only to pass the test of love himself. It is a painful test, as under the penetrating gaze of Jesus he must rise from the death of his egocentricity to a life of utter dependence on the Lord for everything, even for the assurance that he loves Him. How painful it was that his "resurrection" had to be so public.

The response of Jesus was solemnly to appoint this humbled, loving disciple as shepherd over His Flock. Jesus entrusted those whom He loved to a disciple who loved Him. As the Number One Sheep, Peter would have to stay very close to Jesus, listening to His voice and obeying His will (Isaiah 44:28; 1 Peter 5:2–4). The sheep belong to Jesus and always will. In the Old Testament God was the Shepherd of His people, but He entrusted the care of the Flock to Judges, Kings, prophets, etc, to act in His Name. They had divinely delegated authority to rule over the Flock (2 Samuel 5:2–3; 1 Chronicles 17:6), but in obedience to His will, which they had to seek on every occasion (Hosea 4:16; Jeremiah 31:10; Isaiah 40:11).

Peter is Jesus' personal representative. Jesus put the entire mission into his hands. From now on he was to set sail on the sea of life with the other disciples for companions, and bring in the miraculous catch in terms of redeemed persons. The norm for the shepherd is total love for Jesus and for the Flock, who need to be cared for, taught, fed, guided and protected with total dedication and selflessness, even at the cost of the shepherd's life (John

10). Jesus knows that the Flock are safe in the hands of a shepherd who relies on the Lord for everything, one who lives on the level of divine love, where God's solutions for the Flock are made available, rather than just human ones. Jesus can return to the Father happy that the sheep are safe.

This new shepherd must look to the model Shepherd for his direction, and the model Shepherd has laid down his life for the sheep. Peter is now given the challenge to do what he could not have done before. Jesus prophesied a martyr's death for him: " . . . *when you were young you put on your own belt and walked where you liked; but when you grow old you will stretch out your hands, and somebody else will put a belt round you and take you where you would rather not go*." By the time the gospel was written between A.D. 90–95 Peter had been dead about thirty years. Tradition has it that he was martyred by crucifixion in Rome, during Nero's persecution circa A.D. 64–67, as he understood would be his destiny (1 Peter 2:21–23, 4:16). In this way Peter answered Jesus' call to "*Follow me*".

The Beloved Disciple (21:20–23)

This would not be John's gospel if the last word were not given to the Beloved Disciple! Obviously the churches were in a state of flux with the death of the apostles, and by now the Beloved Disciple was dead also, even though he outlived the rest of the Twelve. This led to a rumour that claimed Jesus had prophesied over him too, saying that he would survive until the Second Coming.

This must be dealt with now. John had never denied Jesus, but he was not appointed shepherd of the Flock, so the shepherd position was not given on merit. It was a divine call, and this Beloved Disciple's call was to intimacy with Jesus, and to be one of His most important witnesses, a task he had discharged very well in his gospel. Both Peter and John are witnesses, but called in different ways. Peter was called to "red" martyrdom: John to "white" martyrdom, which is the witness of a long life of total dedication and service to the Lord. We must not compare or say one is more important, when we know that the only important thing is accomplishing the will of God for our lives. The church of John must accept the ministry of the church of Peter and vice versa. There must be no rent in the garment of the Body of Christ, which is woven in one piece from neck to hem by the pure love of Jesus.

Conclusion to the Conclusion

The beloved disciple, who remained faithful to Jesus for the whole of his life, is the authority behind this gospel, and his church is prepared to defend this witness: ". . . *and WE know that his testimony is true*." They have experienced the fruits of believing in Jesus (20:31) and know that He is truly present in their community, but they also know that it is impossible to explain this mystery adequately. Generations of Christians have tried!